The Power of Meaningful Intimacy

The Power of Meaningful Intimacy

Key To Successful Relationships

James C. Crumbaugh, Ph.D., DABPS

Diplomate in Psychotherapy,
American Board of Psychological Specialties

and

Rosemary Henrion, M.S.N., M.Ed., R.N.

Diplomate in Professional Psychotherapy
Fellow and Diplomate in Medical Psychotherapy

Copyright © 2004 by James C. Crumbaugh and Rosemary P. Henrion.

Library of Congress Number: 2003093690
ISBN :   Hardcover   1-4134-1265-3
          Softcover   1-4134-1264-5

All rights reserved. No part of this book may be reproduced or transmitted in any form or by any means, electronic or mechanical, including photocopying, recording, or by any information storage and retrieval system, without permission in writing from the copyright owner.

This book was printed in the United States of America.

To order additional copies of this book, contact:
Xlibris Corporation
1-888-795-4274
www.Xlibris.com
Orders@Xlibris.com

Contents

Acknowledgements 9
Foreword 11
Preface 13
    The Purpose of This Book
Appendix 15
    The Exercises
Chapter I 17
    An Episode To Illustrate The Subject Of This Book ....
    A Once-Over Lightly Of The Entire Scene Of
    Human Motivation . . . . Its Roots In The Sexual Nature
    Of Humankind . . . . How Sex Relates To Developing
    A Meaningful Intimacy Which Creates Success . . . .
    The Seven Steps To Meaningful Intimacy In
    Successful Relationships And Our Technique
    Of Leading You Through Them.
Chapter II 48
    Overall Presentation Of Our Method Of Helping To
    Discover The Hidden Power Of Meaningful Intimacy
    And Life Purpose Within Your Own Brain.
THE SEVEN STEPS TO MEANINGFUL INTIMACY WHICH
LEAD TO SUCCESFUL RELATIONSHIPS

    NOTE: ALL EXERCISES ARE IN THE APPENDIX.
    There will be one or more for each of the seven steps
    except Chapter IV Step 2. Most of the exercises will not

be listed in the Table of Contents; they will be noted at the appropriate place in each chapter with instruction to do the exercise at that time.

Chapter III Step 1 66
Discovering Who You Really Are
Choosing Your View of Life
1. Your view of life's values: The Identity Exercises and the Uniqueness Exercise (Exercise 1); The Role Model Exercise (Exercise 2): the role you choose to play with each sex; The Meaning in Life Evaluation (MILE) Scale (Exercise 3).

2. Choosing your place in the value spectrum from the mechanistic, materialistic and purely objective world to the teleological, intuitive, subjective and *noetic* (or spiritual, though not *necessarily* religious) world. The role of sex in this choice.

Chapter IV Step 2 91
Handling Personal Loss
Grief, disappointment, and the negative feelings which prevent your exploring new life experiences for new meanings: Analyzing your personal history of happy and unhappy experiences: exploring your *status quo* and learning new and better ways of handling your "troubles spots".

Chapter V Step 3 102
Developing Self-Confidence
The Power of Freedom Exercise

Chapter VI Step 4 112
Getting Into the Mind-Set Necessary for Discovery of New Meaning and Purpose
1. Expanding perceptual Awareness (Becoming aware of many variables which passed unnoticed.)
2. Stimulating Creative Imagination (Discovering new meaning in everyday experiences.)

Chapter VII Step 5 118
    Encounter
Chapter VIII Step 6 131
    "Dereflection": Defusing Liabilities and Infusing Assets
        Using the assets you have in spite of all possible handicaps (How to apply the song about "Accent the Positive, Ignore the Negative, and Don't Mess with Mr. In-between" as you set up shop for the Third Millennium.)
Chapter IX Step 7 145
    The Final Scene: "Commitment"
        How to dedicate yourself to your new goals
        1. How to recognize the sexual aspect of goals.
        2. How to uncover, use and recover the sexual roots of goals through meaningful (not sexual) intimacy and thereby establish meaningful relationships.

APPENDIX: The Exercises 159-239
Index 241

Acknowledgements

THE PRODUCTION OF a book is never the work of the authors alone. Behind the scenes many hands and minds operate to make possible the credits (but not the debits!) earned by the writers. In this connection we would emphasize the following:

James C. Crumbaugh, the first writer, extends appreciation to: his family, wife Lois; son Dr. Charles M. Crumbaugh II; housekeeper Jessie R. Lett, who is committed to caring for him and wife; Mark McQuade and Albert J. Henrion, Jr., computer experts who arranged our manuscript into publisher's form. Many friends in the community encouraged the publishing of this work.

Sincere appreciation to friend and colleague, Dr. Robert Barnes, chairperson and professor, Department of Counseling and Human Development, Hardin-Simmons University and President, Viktor Frankl Institute of Logotherapy, who reviewed our manuscript and provided invaluable suggestions for it.

Cannot forget the second writer, colleague for some thirty years who took over my practice upon retirement. She has presented professional papers and workshops in

South America, Europe, Canada, Far East, and the United States describing our program. Rosemary Henrion has magnified the content that she was taught to a much higher level than either could have achieved alone in the **Power of Meaningful Intimacy: Key to Successful Relationships**.

Rosemary Henrion, the second writer, extends appreciation to:

James C. Crumbaugh for his expert mentorship, consultation and collegial relationship. To Albert J. Henrion, Jr., (son) for his administrative expertise in designing professional courses and paper presentations for professional conferences throughout the world. My close relatives, friends and colleagues who encouraged my work in this field, the thousands of clients, combat veterans, special forces, private sector who transcended from the victim level (psyche) to the Human Spirit (survivor) level to make this program a dynamic reality.

Again we would like to extend our sincere appreciation especially to:

Dr. Robert Barnes, who edited our manuscript and provided invaluable recommendations for it.

Foreword

IN THEIR BOOK, **The Power of Meaningful Intimacy: Key to Successful Relationships**, two internationally recognized scholars and practitioners, James C. Crumbaugh and Rosemary Henrion, offer the reading public the benefit to insights from their own remarkably productive careers. Whether you are an academician or layperson, you will find herein their masterful style of writing to be rewarding pleasure, and each carefully constructed exercise an avenue to greater self discovery.

Woven throughout the tapestry of the text is the theory of psychotherapy known as logotherapy which was developed by the late Viktor E. Frankl, MD, Ph.D., of the University of Vienna Medical School. Credited by Frankl for having brought logotherapy into the scientific arena in the United States, James Crumbaugh and his long-time professional colleague, Rosemary Henrion, offer in eloquent style both clinical and empirical evidence of how Frankl's logotherapy helps individuals achieve health through finding meaning and purpose in life.

Throughout the international scientific community, Viktor Frankl is viewed as having rehumanized psychotherapy, and effectively counteracting the cynicism so prevalent in psychology in an earlier part of the Twentieth Century. Indeed, the Twentieth Century embraced both incredible human suffering and equally incredible scientific discoveries.

Even with the threats of terrorism staring us in the face, the

Twenty-first Century holds the promise of the benefits of mankind's pursuit of meaning, truth, goodness, and love. James Crumbaugh's and Rosemary Henrion's landmark publication illustrates the power to be found in meaningful intimacy. This book offers the keys to helping mankind overcome alienation—both on an international and personal basis—and to achieving meaningful intimacy in human relations.

—Robert C. Barnes, PhD
President, International Board of Directors
Viktor Frankl Institute of Logotherapy

Preface

The Purpose of This Book

THE PURPOSE OF the present volume is to offer a plan of self-help to the many people who are struggling in today's fractionated, volatile, fluctuating and unstable society to find something that lasts, something that is worthwhile to latch on to, something dependable over a lifetime, something that gives them a sense of being **SOMEBODY** to somebody, something that gives what the French have called a *raison d'etre* (*reason for living*), and what the Romans called an *apologia pro vita sua* (*apology or justification for ones life, a difference that one lived at all*). We also offer an insight into the challenges of the Third Millennium, which will hold religious meanings for many and strictly secular meanings for others, but which will—if for no other reason than that of *self-fulfilling prophecy* generated by world-wide pockets of anticipation—usher in "a whole new ballgame" in many aspects of life. It will offer new opportunities for all who prepare for the changes to come, the changes which will bud out during the first decade of 2000 A.D. By 2050 A.D. the world will be so different from today that people now would hardly recognize it. But one thing will never change: The power of meaningful intimacy as a conditioner of successful relationships and approaches to the meaning of life.

Our goal is to prepare the reader for both times by a method of finding a **new power of meaningful intimacy** to establish successful relationships in life for all times, and this requires understanding the role of sex attraction in the process.

The present procedures are based on the principles of *logotherapy* (gaining health through finding meaning and purpose in life) created by the late, great Viennese psychiatrist, Doctor Viktor E. Frankl of the University of Vienna Medical School. Underlying these procedures is the role of human sexuality set forth by Sigmund Freud.

It is important to emphasize that logotherapy (and with it the present method) is in no way designed only for "sick" people or people in any sort of therapy; it is rather designed to help the person in the street. That is why we use the term **logoanalysis** instead of **logotherapy**: we are writing, not for mentally "sick" people, but for the everyday person who may "have it all" or only a little, but who senses that there is *more* to life and wants to find it. (Those who are to some degree mentally ill may, however, use this book as ancillary, in consultation with their therapists.)

The first author originated most of the exercises and wrote the text, much of which was taken from his previous books, but in a different context.

The second author replicated and verified the first author's applications, and did the original applications of many exercises which we developed together.

             . —J. C. C.
               Biloxi, MS
                R. H.
           Pass Christian, MS

Appendix

The Exercises

NOTE: UNLESS YOU OWN THE BOOK PLEASE DO NOT WRITE IN IT: MAKE ALL REQUESTED ANSWERS ON SEPARATE NOTEPAPER FOR YOURSELF.

Chapter III Step 1	Discovering Who You Really Are
Exercise 1	The Identity Exercise and the Uniqueness Exercise
Exercise 2	The Role Model Exercise
Exercise 3	The Meaning in Life Evaluation (MILE) Scale: Determining Your Own Basic Values
Chapter IV Step 2	Handling Personal Loss
	There is no formal exercise for this step
Chapter V Step 3	Developing Self-Confidence
Exercise:	The Power of Freedom Exercise
Chapter VI Step 4	Getting Into the Mind-Set Necessary for Discovery of New Meaning and Purpose
Exercise 1	Expanding Perceptual Awareness (Becoming aware of many variables which have usually passed unnoticed)

	Exercise 2	Stimulating Creative Imagination (Discovering new meanings in everyday experiences)
Chapter VII Step 5		"Encounter": Relating to "Significant Others" of Both Sexes
	Exercise 1	Where Are You Now?
	Exercise 2	Easy Start to **Encounter**
	Exercises 3&4	Developing Relationships That Lead to **Encounter**
Chapter VIII Step 6		"Dereflection": Defusing Liabilities and Infusing Assets
	Exercise:	Using Your Assets in Spite of All Possible Handicaps (How to apply the song about "Accent the Positive, Ignore the Negative, and Don't Mess with Mr. In-between")
Chapter IX Step 7		The Final Scene: Commitment
	Exercise 1	Analysis of the New Life Goals to Which You Will be Committed, and Their Sexual Aspects
	Exercise 2	Analysis of Your New Life Goals and Sources of Help in Fulfilling Them As You Uncover the Sexual Roots of All Human Life

CHAPTER I

An Episode To Illustrate The Subject Of This Book.... A Once-Over Lightly Of The Entire Scene Of Human Motivation.... Its Roots In The Sexual Nature Of Humankind.... How Sex Relates To Developing A Meaningful Intimacy Which Creates Success.... The Seven Steps To Meaningful Intimacy In Successful Relationships And Our Technique Of Leading You Through Them.

PERHAPS THE BEST way to introduce the subject of this book is by the following episode representing the first writer's experience:

It was a bad winter night, with heavy spotted rain and some storminess.

My wife and I were visiting another couple, John and Irma. John asked if I ever dated a certain girl before I married and I said, "Yes."

Then he wanted to shock my wife by asking if I ever had intimate relations with the girl.

I returned the shock. "Certainly."

All three slapped an embarrassed look at me. But I continued, "In fact, I've had intimate relations with every girl I've ever dated."

Now the trio really were knocked off balance and showed it, along with an air that it all had to be a joke—obviously because they knew I was no Don Juan.

But I kept on, "Oh, it's true. I've had these relations not only with every girl I've dated, but also with many little girls five or six years old, as well as with their eighty-five and ninety-year-old great-grandmothers."

The three looked at each other with acute embarrassment mixed with shock, and both John and Irma seemed to stumble for words that would excuse one of them to slip out and call the police to pick up one of the raunchy kinkos they'd been reading about.

"Oh, yes," I insisted, "you see I've had sex relations with every woman I've ever met."

By this time they knew they'd have to get me to the nearest mental hospital—fast.

"Let me explain," I smiled, "before you get me lynched. I'm having meaningful intimacy with both of you ladies right now."

My wife jumped up. "Jim's not been well lately. We'd better go." But the rain had increased, and she faltered a bit as she spoke.

I knew I'd better talk fast. "Let me explain from the point of view of the psychologist you know me to be. You see, every time men and women meet socially, they're having social relations, and if they interact **personally** with the opposite sex it becomes a degree of intimacy. Not **sexual intercourse**, certainly, but real intimate relations—and if the relationship is sincere it is **meaningful** intimacy. Of course we don't ordinarily recognize this, but the truth is that sex really is the basis of all social interaction. We may not believe it, but we give ourselves away in the manner in which we dress, groom ourselves, eat at the table, the language we use, the topics we talk about and think about, the styles of our hair, our furniture, our home decor—in fact, in just about everything we have, say and do. Yes, the one force which drives the human 'merry-go-round' is hidden from superficial external or objective view, and we may fail to become aware of it unless we stop to analyze what we are seeing; but when we do study it all, we cannot fail to be strikingly impressed with the fact that—while the bushy part of external leaves representing the human tree covers the branches and much of the trunk, the whole structure is supported and nourished by unseen roots, which are more powerful than any other part of the organism. And in the human organism these roots are related to the instinctive biological drive of reproduction. In ultimate truth this is also correct for all of the fauna and flora of life. Of course these roots lead up to the covered surface which prevents them from being seen as sexual."

By this time the trio had regained some composure, but not necessarily with compatible thoughts.

"Isn't this really Froodism?" John asked.

"You mean Freudism. Yes, Sigmund Freud was the first to demonstrate this in any clear way, only a hundred years ago, for which he was extensively reviled and persecuted, although he neither preached nor practiced the free-love of which he was accused. But now psychologists and psychiatrists can recognize his fundamental contribution without necessarily becoming encumbered by his theories, many of which are very wild, even to his own followers. I certainly am not a follower of these, but I honor his fundamental contributions. He basically wanted to show that in order to understand, predict and control human behavior—which is the goal of psychology—we have to look at the underlying hidden roots of behavior in the instinctive nature of the human organism. Over many thousands of years these roots have grown from erotic sex to meaningful intimacy—like the trunk of a natural tree grows from its roots on the one hand to the branches covered by leaves on the other hand."

Another clap of thunder seemed to punctuate my remarks.

The three had shown considerable relief after my explanation, although even my wife had never heard me go this far, and she was not really at ease. It was obvious that they all thought I had overstepped proper use of sexual terms in order to make a point—a point, incidentally, that they were not sure they bought in the first place.

John broke the remaining tension by remarking, "You seemed to say Frood—Freud—was a psychologist. Wasn't he a psychiatrist?"

"Yes, but he, as well as some other leading psychiatrists, like the late Viktor Frankl, who succeeded him as the 'third school of Viennese psychiatry' (Alfred Adler being the second), often thought of themselves as psychologists. In fact, psychology grew out of psychiatric foundations. A psychiatrist is a medical doctor specializing in abnormal psychology, and these doctors were the early psychologists."

"You're getting in too deep for me," said Irma.

John agreed, "Well maybe you've got a good point in all this—I think it's worth considering. I just never had thought about it all this way—"

"No," I emphasized, "and most people don't. But I think that's why they foul up so many relationships with the opposite sex."

"Well—could be," he reflected somewhat skeptically.

"We've got to go," my wife interjected, sensing a point of breakdown in our meaningful intimacy. "It's getting late, and I know you folks have to be alert in the morning."

"Oh—no," Irma stammered, "it's just—all—so new a way of thinking of these things—"

"I agree," I boosted myself back up a little in her regard, "maybe at a later date we can reflect back over it some—"

The lightning broke into my comment.

"Yeah," John said, "maybe when we've had some time to grind it all through the mill—you do concoct some food for thought. You probably are close to raising the curtain on the 'sexual revolution' of thirty years ago. It would be interesting to see what the teenagers say about these ideas."

"Yes, I'm studying their reactions now, but I don't yet have enough data to comment on their unique attitudes. There is a fan-like spread of feelings among them. But the sexual revolution is now too deeply ingrained in teen and young-adult cultures to go away, regardless of how people view it. We have couples on the extreme right in some colleges who are not allowed to hold hands because of 'what it might lead to.' On the other hand there are colleges where both sexes sleep on the same dormitory floors with no restrictions on cohabitation other than mutual consent—"

The storm continued in my favor, although I was now beginning to wonder if Lois and I would make it home. But I went on:

"The book my colleague and I are writing is designed to get all people to think about the nature of human nature and to understand the way the shadows of sex enter without awareness into all relationships. Couples have to recognize these facts in order to be ready when the facts rear their heads in first arguments. Before the two have settled into the degree and nature of whatever intimacy they are going to have, these hidden sexual factors will emerge. But in order to have a valid relationship the intimacy of any type must have a **meaning**. Whenever you throw your arms around someone you are having a meaningful intimacy if you really mean the hug. It is always related at least indirectly to sex, although not involving sexual intercourse. It puts the two of you in a meaningful closeness, a closeness that is both indirectly sexual and spiritual. Any **closeness** between two human beings is spiritual and expresses love. Intimacy is involved not only in social relations but also in the secondary factors surrounding them— the factors involving the behavior of each with reference to their interaction with other couples and other people in general. This gets at the **meaning** of interaction and the specific purposes stemming from underlying meanings that may design specific behavior patterns. If committed couples can become aware of at least the basics of all of these factors and then devise **together** ways of reacting that will avoid offending the feelings of **either**, this will go a long way toward making their commitment last . . . Well—I didn't mean to lay a lecture on you at this get-together—" Again the rain beat upon the window panes as an excuse for my long-windedness.

"It's been great to be with you," my wife interjected, "you've got to overlook Jim's being immersed in these intimacy things because of this book—"

"It's all right," John said, "as a matter of fact I begin to see the serious side of it; he's on to an important area of human life. I don't know if he's got the answers about how to deal with the conflicts which couples get into . . ."

"I don't expect any commitment to my ideas without people's testing them out for themselves."

"We've really got to run," my dominant half broke in, "and relieve your intimate interpretations of us before we get barred from your list of humanoids altogether."

"Before we leave," I said, "may I add, John, that the girl about whom you asked if I dated—and if I had intimate sex relations—never invited me to bed, and I've never tried to go uninvited."

My wife gave up her frown, and John and Irma had relaxed and started to show us out, and again the storm threatened ominously.

"You'd better wait a little while longer," John said with what I knew was some reluctance.

"Since we're stuck—I mean you're stuck here," Irma said, "tell us a little more about how you teach people to **use** your theory in any practical way."

"I'd hoped you'd ask that. If you have a few minutes more I'll lay it out for you. Yes, I know I've kept you too long already—" There was a clap of thunder, and I took further advantage of the rain.

"The late Viktor E. Frankl of the University of Vienna Medical School gave us in **Man's Search for Meaning** the philosophy of personality I use. He calls his system **logotherapy**, or therapy through finding a meaning and purpose in life. (Greek **logos** can be translated as **meaning**). Everybody has to have a meaning or reason to live or they won't succeed when the going gets tough. The French have called this a *raison d'etre* (reason for living). If you have a powerful reason you can scale mountains. But most people don't have one.

"Frankl lays out an outline of how to go about finding one, but the therapist or counselor and the individual have to improvise the details together. And here the individual is not a 'patient' with a mental illness, but rather an everyday Joe (or Josephine) who has hit a snag and needs help over it. My colleague and I have made a career of helping them to apply Frankl's principles.

"This is done by exploring all of their life experiences to uncover the hidden assets which everyone has in one area or another but which have been suppressed in life's mad scramble, and then by helping them to see ways to use these to create a real life meaning and purpose. In the last analysis real meaning is always **spiritual**—not **necessarily** 'religious' but spiritual in the broad sense of values that relate to the human spirit and bring Joe into closer contact with the true spirit of others.

"In other words, the whole crux in finding a meaning and purpose in life is finding other **beings** (usually people, but also often lower animals—they have 'personalities,' too) with whom to share life's breadth of experience."

"You got it all covered, haven't you? But just how do you get people to find a purpose in life through what you call relationships if they haven't been able to find it in these up to now?"

"By a gimmick which I discovered more than thirty years ago: 'Press On', a slogan and motivating paragraph often seen as a wall plaque. The thrust of it is to recognize that **persistence** and **determination** outweigh education and even talent and genius. Here it is:

> "**Press On**. Nothing in the world can take the place of persistence. Talent will not; nothing is more common than unsuccessful people with talent. Genius will not; unrewarded genius is almost a proverb. Education will not; the world is full of educated derelicts. Persistence and determination alone are all powerful."

"How are you going to get people to believe that? They'd like to, but is it realistic?"

"It is if you give them assignments to test it and they succeed at these. That is what we do."

"What do you mean, assignments?"

"Exercises to perform: some written, and some to act out. Each one is designed to add something positive to the battle of discovering a real cause for which to live—a purpose, based on a meaning which makes one's life distinctive, unique, special—which gives a positive significance to one's having lived at all."

"How long does it take to do all of this?"

"You work at your own speed."

"What if you don't like to do set exercises—what if you get bored or burnt out, or exhausted or to feeling lousy—"

"You don't have to do the exercises if you don't want to. They are designed to help you apply the seven steps to finding this real meaning. We present these steps in simple terms, and you can use the **Press On** principle independently of the exercises to attack each of the steps. Then later—after you begin to feel the success of this principle—you can go back to the exercises if you wish. And we know from experience that most people will want to."

"These seven steps to meaning—you do them all with this **Press On** principle. Who said this first?"

"I don't know. The plaque I bought said that it was anonymous. I have heard it credited to one of the early United States Presidents and also to Ray Kroc who originated McDonald's restaurant franchising.

"But to get back to the steps: you are right, I do them all with this **Press On** principle. I'll just summarize each of them, and you'll see how."

I knew that my talk was already far overtime, but the rain mixed with audible thunder was on my side, so I continued.

"Step One. First, you have to analyze your whole life experience to see what distinguishes you from everybody else. For this step the exercises are simply the recording of demographic data, and the step is easier if you do them. But in any case **determine** to make yourself **persist** until you think you know what distinguishes you from everyone else. And this includes your analysis of your basic life values and your thinking about the main principles of religion and ethics, your basic life style and the kind of life you want to call your own. Here we present some data from a couple of my previous books on these issues, which will analyze the different major views of life and their lifestyles; and we **press** you to choose with **determination** and **persistence** the positions which are right for you.

"Step Two. Then you take up how to handle grief and disappointment in life. We give you principles which various successful counselors have used. If you happen at the time to be in immediate need of this step, of course spend more time here before going on. Again we lead you to **press on** with **determination** until you have gained control over the powerful feelings you will be experiencing. The material we present will help you to do that.

"Step Three. Developing Self-Confidence. If you don't want to do the exercises we show you how to apply the **Press On** principle to **persist** and **determine** to try each day to meet every event of the day with more confidence than you did the previous day—to meet each specific event concerning which you have lacked self-confidence with a new and greater self-assurance than the last time. You'll be surprised at how such an **apparently** over-simplified procedure will soon create a new and definite feeling of improvement.

"Step Four. Getting into the Mindset Necessary for Discovery. You've got to learn how to search out and recognize the experiences that hold the key to the highest level for you. Most people settle for the most obvious ideas and become cops, or reporters or CPAs, and marry superficially, which often works out with great pain. And then, they drift on through life with what they regard as meaning, neither happy nor unhappy, but bored without realizing it. Of course now—in the present 'Age of Divorce'—they part, often angrily, and next time may not bother to marry at all, but just 'sleep around' or cohabitate.

"So to help prevent this and to encourage more lasting marriages we use two gimmicks beyond 'PRESS ON': First we **expand our perceptual awareness** by a daily period of observing some common scene and then making a list of everything we experience, noting the things we haven't seen before. And then we **stimulate our creative imagination** by making up a story about every new thing we've seen. Gradually we build a whole new outlook with many meanings which we have not seen before. For this fourth step it is easier and faster to do the exercises given in the book. But if after looking them over, you prefer to make up some similar procedures, that is also okay.

"Step Five. Encounter: Relating to 'Significant Others'. This is really the primary step for which the others exist. And it is the hardest, whether you follow our exercises or not. The facility with which you do this depends, of course, on your basic personality: Extroverts obviously have an easier time than introverts. But even extreme introverts can 'come out of their shell' following a little practice with our exercises."

I started to ask whether we had better stop here while the rain had subsided, but a flash of lightning and a loud clap of thunder answered the question, and I continued:

"I won't take any time on these exercises; suffice to say that they lead you to interact with others, starting with unthreatening actions like asking a stranger the time, and working up to difficult ones like telling some people you feel a deep affection for them.

"Step Six is 'Diffusing Liabilities.' This means teaching people to 'accentuate the positive, ignore the negative, and don't mess with Mister-In-Between'. Of course this is easier to say than do, but we lead up to it by having people think in detail over every good thing, every asset that they may possibly have (including some they have been overlooking), then every handicap or failure or inadequacy which they have ever had. By showing them that the negative factors do not knock out the positive, and that they still have unused assets which can be called on as a base for new meaning and purpose in life, we demonstrate that all is not as bad as it may have looked at first. And when you do find a real meaning you reach 'significant others'—you stand for something that distinguishes you and appeals to at least some others, who appreciate you because of it. And now you feel like *Somebody*.

"And now finally, Step Seven is the scene which proves your success in all of the other steps, that demonstrates your having found a real meaning and purpose which gives your life value to these others and thus your **certainty** that you are SOMEBODY. But this always requires your being somebody to some other being. We call this step **commitment** because if you have found a real meaning and purpose you will feel drawn to fulfill it in a way which requires your deep and lasting commitment. This is like the commitment marriage is **supposed** to represent.

"Well, the rain seems to have slacked up enough to make our leaving imperative—a good excuse for your pushing us out of the door—"

"Yes—I mean no—that is—" Irma stammered.

"She means—" John broke in, "of course you want out now, but we've enjoyed having you. In fact, your laying out the outline of how you apply the ideas you had been telling us about has made more sense of it all."

"And," Irma added, "when your book comes out we'll buy a copy."

That was the best exit cue a writer could have. I took it.

If you are still with us at this point we will assume that you have grasped the basics of our method, and we will now present the concepts of human motivation which you will need for its execution.

In order to clarify the connection between intimacy and everyday relationships we present below an outline of procedures which you can use in establishing this connection in each type of relationship and in determining your corresponding behavior in relation to it.

Outline of the Easy Way to Analyze All Intimate Relationships

Procedure 1. Analyze the *Type* of Sex Relationship

    a. "Instinctive" sexual activity
        (1). Romantic: "making love", *physical* intimacy
        (2). Personal: deep friendship, but not romantic, may be intimate, but not *physically* so.

    b. Casual
        (1). Occupational (in the workplace)
        (2). Social (all social events)
        (3). "Street" or contact with the mere presence of people (not *emotionally* intimate, but still indirect intimate contact).

      c. Competitional (usually unconscious)
          (1). Occupational competition
          (2). Social competition

Procedure 2. In All Above Relationships *Ask* Yourself: What is the *Sexual* Aspect of this Relationship?

      a. Conscious awareness
          (1). On your part (If you don't at first sense a sexual overtone, visualize the other person as one of the sex opposite to that actually present: what would the relationship then be?)
          (2). On the other person's part (How may that person be visualizing **you**?)

      b. Unconscious (what do you *think may have been* any intimate aspect of which you each have been at first unaware?)

Procedure 3. Analyze the Activity Indicated by this Relationship (What are you **supposed** to say or do?)

      a. Verbal
          (1). "The weather" contact as in an airport with unknown people or as when pausing on the street, and so forth.
          (2). Friendly remark
          (3). "Strictly business" statement

      b. Non-verbal behavior
          (1). "Body language" accepting or rejecting the other.
          (2). Movement toward or away from the other.

Procedure 4. Select Your Appropriate Continuing Attitude or Action in this Relationship Over Time

    a. What you will do *covertly* (in thinking or feeling toward that person over time).

    b. What you will do *overtly* (Here the choices of behavior are too varied and subtle to specify: they will be determined by your already established personality. You may need to experiment, but if you have followed the first three procedures the overt action which best matches your personality will usually become promptly apparent.)

    c. *Covert* as well as *overt* action can be transmitted unconsciously to the other person so keep it "civil".

5. Now: You Are Asking

    a. Surely you don't expect anyone to do all of this in a flash for every contact they make? This is too long a burden even to attempt!

    b. Yes it would be as a constant routine. But here is how you handle that:

        (1). List the previous four procedures in **establishing a relationship** on 3x5 cards for your shirt or coat pocket.

        (2). While you are learning to use them refer to the cards.

        (3). In a short time you will memorize the procedures unconsciously, and they will flash before you in sequence without any attempt on your part. They will no longer be a burden. You will not have to continue even to think of the details of these actions; you will automatically perform them.

In the final analysis achieving a meaning and purpose in life is a journey from sexually intimate love to unselfish intimate love: from what the Greeks have called *eros* to *agape*. The intermediate step between these two is *philia*, the Greek word for "brotherly" love. These three words are used to express the different *kinds* of love. **Meaning** is ultimately an expression of some degree of love in relationship to another Being. This may be a person or a lower animal. While it may also be a **thing** like music or art, relationships other than with a living Being express a **desire** to relate to Beings indirectly. Artists want the world to understand their feelings expressed in art. And the journey to meaning always expresses some form of love action, from *eros* to *agape*. It expresses a reaching out from instinctive *eros* to the higher forms of love, culminating in *agape* or unselfish love. What may seem at first to be selfish love—like music or art—is reaching out to the pleasure of other people, which is one form of *agape*.

There are three levels of *agape*:

Level I. **Casual**, like giving your seat to an elderly person on a subway.

Level II. **Intermediate**: what you do to accommodate friends in spite of your own inconvenience, like offering to furnish the coffee and doughnuts at a club meeting.

Level III. **Supreme**, such as sacrificing one's life for another.

There are many variations and degrees of each of these three levels. For example, Level III may take the form of sacrificing not life and death but of *living* to care for another. This is often more supreme than dying because it may occasion more self-suffering.

A *caveat* should be noted here: **false personal sacrifice** can occur when it does not really help the "loved" one. For example, here is a young girl who lost her lover in military action. She never married because of his memory: no one else could ever come even close to his perfection as she remembered it. Actually she "Christophied" him. Experiments have shown that we generally forget more unpleasant things and recall the more pleasant ones. She continued to believe him perfect. She lived out her life this way, and died virtually alone, whereas a more realistic appraisal of his memory would have permitted her to accept another suitor and to rear a secure family.

Most marriages reach only **High Intermediate** *agape*: they aren't perfect, but mates who are truly seeking and experiencing a genuine commitment come to accept and adjust to imperfections. This brings them into a **High intermediate** relationship; then if the need for supreme sacrifice occurs, **supreme** *agape* is likely to follow. A Rabbi of our acquaintance said that a large number of his pre-marriage counselees say of the mate they have selected, "This isn't altogether what I wanted, but it is probably the best I can do." So they make do with that; and the Rabbi says most of these marriages last.

Once again, **supreme** *agape* can in some cases take a very **vicious** turn, as when the "sacrifice" is really a selfish desire to *control* the life of the person for whom the sacrifice is made. This is often a form of "sacrificial" selfishness, which feeds the ego of the sacrificer while destroying all independence of the object of sacrifice. A parent may feel saintly while ruining the child's ability to behave independently in a competitive world. Parental control in early years is really needed and has sagged badly in the last two generations in America; but there must be a cap on this control which prevents stifling the child's personality.

Another prime example of false *agape* in this **intermediate** Level II is seen in the typical "Hollywood" society. For example, Zsa Zsa Gabor addresses casual contacts as "Dawling" to get them to believe she really cares about them, whereas she really wants them to boost her reputation.

Observations of obviously false behavior lead many people, including many scientists, to conclude that true unselfishness really does not occur. But examination of many opposite actions will show the opposite type of motivation—and sometimes even in the Hollywood atmosphere. As a society we need to restore family commitments in order to restore the concept of true and lasting **commitment** of married couples and thus to rehabilitate American family life. This will do more than anything to restore the true meaning of *agape* in the lives of the American people.

The present historically unique war against *Terrorism* points up both the need for *agape* and the opportunity to create it. On September 11th, 2001, we saw in the streets of New York City multitudes of expression of **intermediate** *agape*, whereas even the casual *agape* of common civility has long been a seldom experienced luxury there. In the past, one has been tempted to conclude that because New Yorkers are rude (which they are) they are also heartless (which they are not, as shown by the street behavior on September 11th). We should say a further word about the mechanistically-oriented behavioral scientists who claim that true *agape* does not exist: *All* behavior—even mother love, they say—is selfishly motivated. To support the latter they resort to an argument which seems absurd to most of us, namely, that such behavior is really only to aid the passing on of the behaving organism's genes! The present writers would conclude that the September 11th behavior of New Yorkers cannot be adequately explained by any other concept than that of *agape*.

The mechanists or "reductionists" (who say all behavior and experiences are *reducible* to **physical** concepts) simply define *agape* out of existence, by saying we always do what we want to do physically, regardless of conscious feelings. We may choose "good" or "bad", but whatever we do we will have *chosen* to do, within the limits of our physical capabilities. Our behavior may either benefit or hurt another, but in any case we will have chosen to do what we want to do.

Perhaps so, *but some people choose to do what benefits* **them**, *while others choose to do what causes them great suffering in order to help someone else*. All choose to do whatever they do, but their motivation is very different. The second kind of behavior is true *agape*.

Yes, *agape* does exist and is the ultimate goal of all true love. And—contrary to first impressions—all love including that between father and son, mother and daughter, sister and sister, brother and brother is really sexual, because all relationships have a sexual component. Though they do not involve **physically** sexual behavior they represent feelings and attitudes which stem from sexual roots. Therefore in dealing with all relationships you will be more successful by evaluating the intimate factors through the outline of these factors which we have presented.

If you've got everything you want in life you don't need our—or anyone else's—help. But if you have everything you're the rare exception. After our careers in hospitals, clinics and counseling centers we have learned what most people want, and how they screw up their attempts to get it by trying for right goals the wrong way, or by trying for wrong goals the right way. And for a combined period of more than two generations we have helped many hundreds of people to set their sights on what they **really** want out of life and how to get it.

No matter what you want out of life you have to have a reason for wanting it. You have to have a purpose for living, a **reason** for struggling at all. The French have called it a **raison d'être,** a reason for being; the Romans called it an **apologia pro vita sua,** an apology for your life. Otherwise we get bored, and every frustration constitutes a challenge to wanting to go on. George Sanders, one of the top movie actors of a generation ago, being retired in Spain, wrote a note that "I'm bored", and checked out. The late great psychiatrist, Viktor E. Frankl of the University of Vienna Medical School (**Man's Search for Meaning**), called this "existential vacuum", which inevitably leads us to severe trouble. Maybe we turn to drugs, or to promiscuous sex, or to anti-social behavior from fist fighting to violent crime. Leo Rosten (the author of **Captain Newman, M.D.**) had Newman say, "The purpose of life is to count, to make a difference that you lived at all." Orville Kelly, a journalist, found he was dying of cancer. He didn't give up but instead recognized that Capt. Newman was right. He founded a club by the name, **Make Today Count**. He did eventually die of cancer, but he had some years during this period in which he was very productive in leading this club. Enzo Stuarti was a popular singer in the Sixties. At every performance the audience was deeply moved, and someone would almost always ask, "Surely you don't work this hard every time you sing, do you?" He replied, "Yes I do, because no one has promised me tomorrow, and I want today to count."

We have to have a real life meaning, like Beethoven's music (or even Elvis Presley's), or Picasso's art, or maybe even the best artist in the elementary school you attended, or Bill Gates' Microsoft, or Michael Jordan's basketball, or Tiger Woods' golf, or bowling champ on your office's team, or John Barrymore's acting, or the lead in the senior play of your high school class or the local leading amateur astronomer, or amateur magician, or a local church choir's organist, or Gypsy Rose Lee's strip teasing, or the local tango champion, or the yo-yo champ in your neighborhood, or the best imitator of Dolly Parton.

Or: if you cannot be the best, you may be tempted to be the worst, one who can kill the most people from The University of Texas Tower, or the most in a Colorado grade school, or commit the most atrocious mass murder of the century. If we cannot be the best of a socially desirable goal, we may be strongly tempted to be the worst of a socially reprehensible goal. But we'll be a contender—a Somebody in some social millieu if we can. And through all of the negative or anti-social achievements we will fail to see—or see too late—that we could have had a far better life in the "right" or humanly beneficial life style if we'd gone about it differently, and that the satisfaction would have been far greater in the long run.

Yes, you **can** achieve true and rewarding goals in life if you latch on to the **Power of Passionate Purpose in establishing meaningful intimacy**—and you **can** latch on if you go about it right. That's what this book is all about.

Actor Kirk Douglas said, "It is easy to find meaning in life—just stand for something." Very good, Mr. Douglas. But you need to stand for something that brings you the **true** rewards which human beings through the ages have wanted—such as those illustrated by Enzo Stuarti, Babe Ruth, Mickey Rooney, Pablo Picasso, Frank Sinatra, all of whom found great meaning in their work, and not in the socially destructive goals that separate you further from true meaning and leave you embittered, half alive and in shambles. It is very important in choosing life goals to ask of each one, Will this bring me appreciation from my "significant others" (a term for those important to you), or could it end with the opposite result?

Yes, we know, one person's good goal is another's boredom: One who is talented in math may pursue life purpose as Einstein did, but one who hates math may be tempted to escape its boredom by anti-social behavior if he or she cannot find a satisfactory substitute. If you really look, however, a good substitute is available.

It is further said that there is something for everybody in which he/she can be superior. Unfortunately this is not always true: The fact is that a relatively few people in any area of life have most of the talents, while the majority of us ordinary people have few if any talents above average. So how can such people find meaning?

Is there any hope for them? Yes indeed, there is a lot of hope. Now competition under the capitalist laws of supply and demand has served the human race historically best—though only when there are some umpires and referees to keep it all fair and above board. Even so there will always be many who cannot compete successfully. Not just the anti-social people we have been describing—they usually find competitive success, although at the price of tragic results in the long run.

So what **can** "everyday" people of modest abilities do to find coveted meanings and purposes in today's ultra-competitive world? They may not have talent for anything, but one can succeed to a satisfying degree in many varied areas of endeavor without it. How? By two processes: (1) Understanding the basic intimate nature of human motivation and how to handle this covert fact in overt society and (2) following one basic proverbial rule.

Let us take the rule first. It is given on a plaque on the senior author's office wall.

Yes, we've already given this in the Introductory Episode which outlines our overall procedure, but now we have to become more specific.

It sounds too simple to work—but it will if applied correctly. We are going to teach you step by step how to put this plaque into practice. It can lead you not only to find a truly rewarding meaning and purpose in life, but also to experience success where you had known or expected only failure. If on the other hand you usually succeed it can still help you to much greater success. No, you won't become a genius if you aren't one already. You won't achieve talent if you don't already have it. And if you don't have the education you want, it won't educate you. But you won't have to have genius, talent and high education to experience success in life. With that success you may also achieve education, but it **per se** will not be the cause of success. You would have to get **training** to be a barber or a teacher, a lawyer or an engineer or a doctor. But the highly trained person may not be educated. And if you pursue the plan we are going to lay out for you, you may well become able to get training in a field of your desire. There are many other objectives for which you can get training on the job or "in the field". And there are many self-taught hobbies, from physical education to amateur cosmology, from amateur astronomy to hot air ballooning, from robotics to falconry—and don't forget the pets. Dogs and cats furnish meaning to multitudes.

All right, now let's review this plaque on the first writer's office wall; again we do not know the source of it, as it has been attributed to several different origins. The slip that came with the plaque says that it is anonymous.

PRESS ON.

Nothing in the world can take the place of persistence. Talent will not; nothing is more common than unsuccessful people with talent. Genius will not; unrewarded genius is almost a proverb. Education will not; the world is full of educated derelicts. Persistence and determination alone are all powerful.

Sounds too simple and obvious? And again how are you going to persist—haven't you already been doing that without studying this paragraph? Not the way we're going to teach you, you haven't. No, it doesn't mention meaningful intimacy but as the story unfolds you'll see that its message involves this concept.

Of course **Press On** does not mean that talent has no place in success. It is foolish to persist in a musical career if you are tone deaf as is the first author. But believe it or not—the following is a true story: In the deep depression of the Thirties he had to have a teaching job. He had played the single reeds strictly by note, but someone else had to tune the instrument for him as he could not match the pitch pipe. Now in teaching he was assigned to the origin and development of a school band in this very primitive country combined campus of grade and high school, because the music teacher was on leave. And believe it or not, this writer taught both reeds and brass (he never played the latter in his life); and by the end of the year he had a little marching band which was playing for the ball games. No, it wasn't any champion musical group, but it passed muster in this primitive situation, **purely the result of Pressing On Now with Persistence And Determination (PON** with **PAD)**. Again he would have been foolish to have tried to become a professional musician, but with motivation you can reach some degree of success without talent when you have to do so. By watching for opportunities and sometimes making them where they don't exist, you can achieve goals you didn't expect to be possible. Yes you can, many, many times when you think you can't. You can by **PON** with **PAD**.

We are going to lead you through the application of this technique. But first let's analyze human motivation enough to let you see where you stand in it, and where you may need to stand in order to apply the technique.

Earlier we said that people without talent, every day folks and even those who seem to have no assets on their side can succeed by this **PON** with **PAD** rule plus understanding the basics of human motivation. Now let's look at the underlying principles of motivation.

Motivational Analysis shows us where we are now. **Discovery of Meaning and Purpose in Life** will show us where we need motivation to go in order to fulfill the meaning.

Motivation is the push toward meaning and purpose that will challenge us to do our best and to counteract the mental, physical and emotional blocks or obstacles that have been causing failure or at least lessening our achievement by obscuring our true ability to achieve.

Intentionality (or "will power"): Motivation enables the power of finding meaning, whereas **intentionality** enables the power to achieve purposive goals which will fulfill this meaning.

The exercises in this book are simple and are designed to help you establish your uniqueness and with it the opportunities to be found in this uniqueness—opportunities which are never shared in the same extensity and degree with any other human being. Again they do not presuppose talent or genius, or immediate education beyond what you now have. When this uniqueness is fully understood, you will know the true nature of your motivation, and this will enable the culling of weak and ineffective methods of adjustment to conflict and the emphasis upon other methods which have a good chance of success.

Now back to intimacy: What is the sexual nature of all of this? The answer will unfold as we employ the plaque. There we will see how pressing on with persistence and determination involves persistence in work that takes us into interaction with the opposite sex, and how this interaction plays a major part in achieving what we are determined to get. In the long run we gain very few goals in life which are not covered by an undercurrent of sexual interest.

If sex is so important in everything as it seems to be from everything we see on the TV and hear all around us, just how do I specifically learn to handle all of the everyday life conflicts between the sexes, which could fill all of the books on legendary intimacy ever written? Don't I have to deal with these in order to activate your plaque's "Press On" technique? Yes, indeed you do. And if, after our pointing these up you are aware of some deficit here, we are going to teach you how to proceed in dealing with it.

You may also find some help from popular books by such names as Abigail Van Buren, Ann Landers, Dr. Joyce Brothers and so forth. And Books-A-Million, Borders, Bookland, Waldenbooks and Barnes and Nobles are some of the sources. *But there is a caveat here: these popular advisors select cases that fit their own concepts which may or may not fit your specialized situation. Evaluate each case with care—and, if you have any professional advisors in mental health care, with their opinions in mind.*

Here is a "once over lightly" outline of the whole motivational scene.

Unsuccessful or Escape Mechanisms of Adjustments to Conflict

1. Projection

Projection is blaming others for our own failures, or blaming circumstances which have caused us to be unsuccessful, circumstances over which we supposedly have no control. We may really have no control of the circumstances, but we always do have control of the **attitude** which we take toward dealing with these circumstances. We always have a choice of two different basic attitudes:

> a. We can give up and blame our misfortune for failure. In this case we are already whipped because we have quit trying.

> b. Or we can take the **positive attitude** of accepting the fact that if we quit we will then be whipped completely, whereas if we go on and do the best we can in spite of these circumstances we do have a chance to accomplish **something**.

2. Rationalization

This is the false reasoning which we make as excuse for failures and the claim to ourselves and others that we have really not failed because this is the only way things could have been. There are several different patterns which rationalization can take. The literature often describes them under the following terms:

> a. "Sweet Lemon"

This is the attitude of accepting failed circumstances but claiming that they are really what we wanted in the first place. For example, we buy a car which turns out to be a "lemon", but we take the attitude that it really is the car we wanted anyway.

> b. "Sour Grapes"

This is the well-known attitude of justifying failure by saying that the goal really was a poor one in the first place. For example, we try out for a certain job without success, so we make the excuse that it was really a very poor opening in the first place.

c. "Suffering Hero"

We endure failure to achieve a desired goal, and claim that we poured so much emotional as well as physical energy into working toward it that we really have reached a position of exhaustion. But we surround ourselves with feelings of having tried nobly to achieve a socially desirable goal, and that we deserve great credit for now having to endure the impossible. Here again we must not be allowed to claim to be a "victim" of circumstances beyond our control. Once again the **attitudinal value** (the term of the famous psychiatrist, the late Viktor Frankl of the University of Vienna Medical School) must be called into use. We've already noted the importance of taking the positive attitude toward all circumstances of failure as described under **Projection**.

d. "Logic-Tight Compartments"

Often people become aware of a discrepancy between behavior in one area of personality and that in another. This discrepancy creates a conflict which they escape by compartmentalizing their thinking. That is, they will not think of both at the same time, but rather will seal each off into a separate cognitive compartment with care not to let the two into conscious experience at the same time. This is an altogether unconscious process; if they were consciously aware of what they were doing they would be in deep mental conflict. But "repression into the Unconscious" is a well-known mental phenomenon which was first described by Sigmund Freud over a hundred years ago. For example, a person may have an extra-marital affair, and at the same time be aware of the marital vows. The clash between this inconsistency is avoided by sealing the two sets of thought processes off as above described.

This "logic-tight compartments" form of rationalization often gives immediate relief from conflict, although in the long run it never succeeds. It is much more dangerous to overall mental health than the several forms of rationalization described before it. And because it is so very sensitive to inconsistent behavior it requires more careful attention than the other types of rationalization.

3. Anxiety

In today's supposedly civilized life, most of us live under considerable pressure (for example, resulting from having to work at one or maybe two jobs and then coming home to care for the family) and therefore anxiety is greatly experienced by almost everyone. It is, of course, a nervous reaction to emotional stress. While no one can escape all of it, an essential feature of better adjustment today requires that we find time for relaxation and "letting off steam".

4. Depression

Depression is another psychological state which today's ultra-competitive society forces upon almost all of us at one time or another. There are different levels of depression and different types. One type occurs as a severe mental illness, usually requiring hospital treatment, but the more common variety is the everyday type resulting from the stress of modern living. This usually passes with time. Psychiatric consultation and medication will usually be necessary for severe depression, but today's society is far over-medicated and over-treated for conditions which our ancestors took in stride as part of life. (Yes, they had stress too, although they usually had much better periods of relaxation between points of stress. The pressure of fighting Indians with one hand while caring for the baby with the other certainly equaled anything we have today, but for the most part the whole of life offered much better interludes of recovery from such stress.)

5. Obsessive-Compulsive-Disorders

Under this condition we have some extreme patterns of handling every little detail of the day's work with a fine toothed comb, which allows no deviation from perfection. We are obsessed with work—or with play, with whatever we do. And we are compelled toward this state of perfection which nobody can really achieve.

Here are included phobias, which are "false fears". Now such fears must be distinguished from rational fears, such as fear of a Cobra snake. If the object of fear really is a danger, it is not a phobia. But many times we are seized with fears that have no rational basis because they involve things which really cannot hurt us. For example, perhaps the most common is what is called **claustrophobia**: We are afraid of closed spaces like elevators, or closets. Another very common phobia is **agoraphobia**: The fear of open spaces. For example, we may be afraid to go outdoors, and therefore we cannot get to work. In these cases there's always a psychological reason for the fear: In some way it enables us to escape something which is unpleasant and for which we have found no adequate adjustment. Agoraphobia is often motivated by an unconscious desire to escape some situation—like an unpleasant aspect of the job we have—and which situation we can escape if we are unable to go outside to work.

6. Hypochondriasis

This is excessive concern with personal conditions of health and well-being. We take every "patent" medicine on the drug store shelf and we hound our doctors to prescribe everything which we can't get "over the counter". This usually is a result of personal fear of some life situation which recedes into the background as long as we are fully occupied on the conscious level by medical and health problems.

Successful Techniques of Adjustment

1. "Direct Attack"

This is always the best procedure if it can be used. That is, look at the situation rationally, see what needs to be done, and proceed directly to carry this out. Unfortunately, most situations of real conflict are not so easily handled. Therefore we must look to the next best procedure:

2. Compensation

When we fail to achieve one goal, we compensate by achieving another. For example, we fail to get one job, but we compensate for this failure by obtaining another one of equal value.

3. Sublimation

Sometimes we cannot find an adequate direct substitute for a desired goal, so we have to sublimate this desire by interest in other goals which are not direct fulfillments of the same need as the sublimated goal but which do give us the same degree of feeling of success as the unattainable goal. For example, the priest in the Roman Catholic church must remain celibate, but he directs the energy that others give to a family into the service of such other families. As has become apparent in recent years, some can do this while others can't, and failure may not be manifested in training years. Sublimation must be carefully self-observed, and changed where it begins to fail. Other forms of sublimation can be tried. Success may require a change in vocation or environment.

Now maybe you recognize yourself in one or more of these faulty mechanisms of adjustment which we have described. Hopefully you will be able to claim use of at least one of the "good mechanisms" of adjustment. To the extent that you are in the faulty column you may be able to lift yourself out by the **"PON with PAD"** technique. **(PRESS ON NOW with PERSISTENCE AND DETERMINATION.)** But if you sense that you have several of these mechanisms or any one of them to a severe degree you should go to a mental health professional for an evaluation.

With this history of human motivation in mind you are ready to proceed with application of our technique. We'll start you off very simply and gradually with minor everyday problems. We'll build up to the tough everyday problems that you will face. As you study it, you will be asked to apply it step by step to everyday difficulties. You will work at your own pace, but the more time and effort you can give to it now, the faster you can complete the program. There are seven steps to a new mission and meaning in life. The sooner you can complete the **seven steps**, the sooner you can find the form of sex which can give the meaning that will become your passion for life in the Third Millennium.

In the next chapter we will detail more of our **method** in order to prepare you for our seven steps. You will be making some important applications of **Press On** in advance of the steps. This will enable you to carry them out more easily.

CHAPTER II

Overall Presentation Of Our Method Of Helping To Discover The Hidden Power Of Meaningful Intimacy And Life Purpose Within Your Own Brain.

BEFORE WE GO further, let us be more specific on the one thing which often unobtrusively but always presently infiltrates our actions: the hidden power of sex. If we now examine the "raw" side of sex to the extent that it operates before necessarily becoming obvious, we will be able to see its subliminal action and other everyday actions; we will be able to handle it effectively without either overstepping or underrating the process. Meaningful intimacy may or may not induce sexual intercourse or "raw sex", but it always has sexual overtones.

Sex is the strongest biological drive except hunger. Natural law obviously designed each human being to express sexual intercourse and to beget children from at least shortly after puberty until the menopause (which—unknown to most people—does involve both sexes although in a different way). Sexual intimacy may be enjoyed far beyond menopause. In fact the female often enjoys sex more after the menopause because there is no longer any fear of pregnancy. The question then becomes one of moral and social values, including the dictates of religion and the mores (behavior patterns which the culture considers necessary) of the society to which the individual belongs.

Now let's go back to the first and see how sex was generally regarded. In most tribal and early cultures males were considered adults at puberty, as attested by the Hebrew **bar mitzvah**. (There is also a parallel ceremony for females at the beginning of the teens. It is the "gift" of adult independence and responsibility from the parent to the next generation.)

Historically the young people were supposed to be qualified to begin a new life. The male had already learned much of his father's trade and was ready to assist him in making a living. Or if the boy were not so fortunate he would apprentice himself to someone else—enough to live on. And the girl had learned the family rights and rituals and the skills expected of her. If not very skilled, she soon learned after marriage, and because all life was primitive and comparatively simple, lengthy training was not ordinarily necessary.

There was little time from fourteen to nineteen—much less from nineteen to perhaps twenty-five—during which boys were in **training** to make a living; they were expected to function as above indicated. During all of this time the male's sex-related glands were pumping out the strongest human hormones other than those for hunger. The female's processes are less easily aroused, but when they are they can challenge the best males.

Jesus lived, worked, taught and behaved in a very different world from that of today. We can only reason about what he would say about today's situation, or infer it from Scriptures which were written in ancient times. Reasoning apart from Holy Scriptures would dictate a need for revaluation in terms of conditions today. And such revaluation would strongly suggest that today's rules are correctly modified **at least to some degree** from the classical religious and/or traditional views of a hundred years ago, or even of sixty years ago, much less than from two thousand years ago. The essential question now is **how much** modification is best? Have we overstepped? Or are we on course?

The essence of these earlier years was prohibition of sexual intimacy—and certainly of intercourse—until marriage. "Nice girls" did not permit intimate bodily contact—and "nice boys" did not demand this of them—until the marriage vows were sealed. These mores were not enforced as strictly against males as against females (most likely because pregnancy would reveal feminine violation), but the principles applied to both.

Now of course many American sub-cultures still demand these principles, at least in theory. But something happened to modify them in the overall patterns of behavior which can be considered the nearest representation of an overall American culture. And **some** change seemed necessary to adjust the biological nature of the human organism to the vastly changed economic situation which required longer and longer periods of training before one could function adequately to make a living.

There were signs of change in the sixties, but in the seventies the essence of what has come to be called the **"sexual revolution"** became sufficiently wide-spread to be recognized as a definite change in the sexual mores of American culture. It was pretty generally "across the board" in American society as a whole, in spite of the resistance of some powerful sub-cultures.

And the changes were not—as one might suppose—primarily the result of male efforts; they were rather initiated by female action to modify the status of women and to set themselves as equal in all respects to men. **"Women's Lib"** and sexual equality became key concepts as the younger women revaluated their status and considered that there is no more logic or ethics in holding them to virginity before marriage then in holding men to celibacy—which they knew was not generally done. They knew that if men were required to observe this standard most would still surreptitiously violate it and try to get the girls to violate it, because the males still would not be as easily caught.

So—the new female teen-ager and young woman were created. This sexual change has become so pervasive and apparently accepted or at least tolerated by the majority of the past generation of both sexes, and endorsed and generally practiced by the present younger generation of both sexes from seventeen to thirty—that it is hard to expect any reversal in the foreseeable future.

And yet with all of the changes the essence of femininity is still materialized today as in early times as that of the protective mother who is unfulfilled either by "sleeping around" or short-term commitments, or by a life alone. Witness the number of "single mothers" who have children, who have chosen to marry and then to divorce with children whom they now consider mostly their own; or to arrange short-committed live-together without marriage, and then to have babies who will be theirs with or without father-support; or to adopt other children from various cultures. "Human nature" is still (and we believe always will be) family-oriented, except that now the definition of family has been changed. Now we have the question of whether homosexual couples can rear children. What is a family?

This means that as you choose your sexual attitudes for the future the **traditional** as well as the **unorthodox** must be considered in the choice. You do need to know the history behind the changes in order to assess them for this choice.

The first great change in the intolerant sexual mores of the Victorian Era occurred simultaneously with the advent of Sigmund Freud (though most of the popular interpretations of Freud were false sensationalism accusing him of violations of the then current moral code, which violations he never taught) and of World War I (which, like all wars, loosened sexual restraints). The "flappers" and "jelly beans" of that era gained acceptance of "necking" and "petting" as long as "it stopped there."

Then World War II caused the second marked loosening of these same mores in a practical rather than a theoretical way: the "as long as it stopped there" was still theoretically expected, but the majority of "nice girls" who felt "really in love" would at least occasionally accept their lovers' advances by going with them to a motel for several hours.

A little pattern of behavior was typical. The couple would drive up to the motel; the girl would hold her hand bag up to hide her face; the man would go in and register as Mr. and Mrs. John Jones and pay for the night since they had no luggage; he would take the two keys and drive his car into the slip reserved for that room and then both would go in. No one checked when they left—except some home-owned motels where the male-owner would rent the room for a couple of hours for a reduced fee; and when the couple left would have the assistant change the sheets and would start looking for the next couple. On the contrary there were some owners who refused to rent to anyone with a car having a local license plate. So there was a wide difference in local acceptance of this behavior, but there were few even small towns where a couple could not find a haven anywhere. Now this pattern is by no means gone today although it is seldom needed, because most hotels and motels now will ask for only one responsible registrant, and how many others will share the room, often charging for the number without reference to their sex.

The pendulum of strong changes in mores always eventually swings back, but it never swings all the way back. At least some of the changes will remain. Some of the sexual revolution will become a part of any future modified sexual mores. The most daring bikinis of today may grow into more modest forms, but the bikini will be here. Some prognosticators are saying that within several years prime time television will accept full frontal nudity of both sexes. This may or may not be a correct prediction, although at some future point mixed nudity will very likely be accepted in the same way that present-day scanty bathing suits compare to the full skirt and leg-cover swimming apparel of the twenties. As a matter of fact, nudist colonies do not manifest much sexual behavior. It is not the human body but the human mind that leads us into trouble.

So where do you stand? As we previously indicated, your choices of sexual behavior must be based on your deepest personal values; and the MILE form—the **Meaning in Life Evaluation** to which we have previously referred—will help you to choose the types of behavior you accept and those you reject, and then more specially to formulate the over-all lifestyle which most closely conforms to your total pattern of values.

Oh, you're way ahead of us? You're married and have your life already worked out? Fine.

Or you are divorced, and your new life is well adjusted? Sixty years or two generations ago divorce was tolerated but not accepted in the basic mores of America. Now it is established in the moral code by the fact that nearly half of American marriages end in divorce. If you've been through all of this with a good adjustment, fine. But if the adjustment has not been so good you may find our method of looking for meaningful intimacy just what you need.

You may need to go on for a chapter or so before you will feel like there is a new road to the future. Any time you wish, you can always toss the book in the wastebasket. Maybe you will later reconsider and pull it out before the garbage man comes. If not, we will survive with those whom we have helped in the past and who have told us so. But we will always be interested in you and hope you will find all of the answers. If you're now still with us (as most of those who have started with us have been), you are now ready for Chapter III, Step 1. But read on: There are some points to stress before you enter upon the steps.

Coming this far means you are not—in spite of the successes you may have had—fully satisfied with your present position and status in life, that you want something more, but are not sure how to get it. You want a competitive edge. Now neither this nor any other book can get it **for** you. But we **can** help you to get it for yourself. We know this because we have successfully used the material herein over many years, and (while neither this nor any other method works 100% for everyone) we are certain that it works for the vast majority of those who actually **try** to put it into practice. If you really want help and are willing to give us a chance to demonstrate the value of our **Method** by full participation in it, the results will make you glad you did.

To get down to the "nitty-gritty" of it all, as we have already told you, we will work with you through a series of time-tested exercises which will take you step by step (seven steps altogether) in discovering the goals which will satisfy your needs, and which are often unconscious. Then we will help you discover the (again often hidden) assets and abilities that you have to satisfy these needs. This **Method** will aid you in finding the road (often rocky and seldom traveled, but a lot easier with a "guide" through the forest) to specific immediate goals that are practical in your case.

In addition to the exercises which accompany the steps for each chapter we have constructed a parallel pattern of **ACTIONS** which will show your immediate success in each step, and which give you a chance to go back and "reorganize" any steps that you have not fully achieved.

We will present these **ACTIONS** first, as they will be with you from now on until you have reached fulfillment of your chosen goals and have gained success in achieving your dominant life values.

The **ACTIONS** stem from this plaque which the senior author has on his office wall (already referred to twice in Chapter 1), and which he has come over many years to regard as a **necessity** in accomplishing **any** goal, even though success may be greatly aided by other factors (to be discussed later). We offer it again because it is used as a key factor in our **Method**:

> **PRESS ON**
>
> NOTHING IN THE WORLD CAN TAKE THE PLACE OF PERSISTENCE TALENT WILL NOT; NOTHING IS MORE COMMON THAN UNSUCCESSFUL PEOPLE WITH TALENT. GENIUS WILL NOT; UNREWARDED GENIUS IS ALMOST A PROVERB. EDUCATION WILL NOT; THE WORLD IS FULL OF EDUCATED DERELICTS. PERSISTENCE AND DETERMINATION ALONE ARE ALL POWERFUL.

Working through these **ACTIONS** represents the **mechanics** of finding your fundamental life meaning and purpose in facing the Third Millennium. Applying them to your daily life develops your **motivation** to follow the mechanics. Here are the actions and their meanings in our context. Read through all of them carefully before starting to use them. They are presented below in the usual order of application to each of the exercises as described in each of the **seven steps** in finding meaning in life (each **step** being given in one of the **chapters** in the book).

As you consider each action remember that all actions have *some relationship to meaningful intimacy. As you select a daily problem (later) to handle through these actions you must ask yourself the direct or indirect, subjective or objective nature of this intimate factor, and what* **attitude** *toward the relationship will harmonize with the factor.*

We cannot emphasize too much the **daily** repetition of **PRESS ON**. It is a good idea to write the following four actions consecutively on a 3x5 card and check off each one as it is reached. A new card will be needed for each new goal you choose.

Now let's take an example:

Each morning as you arise and prepare for the day utilize the following four actions:

Action 1. Think of some **problem** or **situation** which you would like to handle during the day: maybe interaction with the boss or spouse or child or co-worker. In any event note the relation to meaningful intimacy, overt or covert, which you believe is involved. Then consider how you can best handle this factor to gain your objective with the problem.

Action 2. Think of how you would like the problem to be resolved, but also the probable arguments given by your opponent for a different outcome.

Action 3. Think of yourself carrying out your own resolution but with the *caveat* of listening to the other side and reasoning about any modification thereby derived.

Action 4. Say to yourself the **Press On** paragraph.

As you prepare the morning activities including breakfast and grooming, if you have to leave for work or other activity think through these four **actions** several times. Then during the day proceed to apply the four above actions as best you can. In the evening reflect on how well you did. If well, congratulate yourself and choose another problem for tomorrow. If not well, ask yourself why, and repeat the overall procedure tomorrow.

If you failed today **don't be discouraged. Nobody wins 'em all.** If you can't shake worry over it go on with another problem tomorrow, but come back to the preceding one as soon as you can—don't let yourself "off the hook" by ceasing to try it. But try **another easier** problem for tomorrow.

Try until you succeed well with a problem. Then you'll get the **feel of success**, and from there on it will all be easier—and then it is time to return to any failed problems.

Does this whole procedure seem too hard? Too primitive or too obvious to work? We have had some who thought one way or the other at this point, but those who persisted to the **feel of success** began to perceive it all in a new light: It really does work to handle problems that were previously too difficult to tackle. We know it will work for you if you will work at *it*.

We know from experience that most who feel that it won't work are really concerned that they may not be equal to the task of making it work. At this point it can all look rather foreboding—like a rather formidable job to enter on just because the writers of a book say it will work. We can understand your position. But listen to this story about how you can test our method in a very simple way.

The myth of *The Tortoise and The Hare* will illustrate the main point: The rabbit, feeling superior, was over-confident and wasted time in his race with the turtle, thinking that the latter had no chance and therefore could be ignored. But by **PAD** (Persistence And Determination) the old slow-mover kept a steady speed, and before the rabbit knew what happened he was defeated. The fact that this fable transcends the ages shows that the principle has been recognized ubiquitously.

This is not to say that native capacities (**TAG** or Talent And Genius) cannot be important in success. If you're fortunate enough to have them you are in a position for S—S (super-success). But if you lean on these superiorities, as the rabbit leaned on his speed, you are likely to lose in the long run just as he did. You would probably feel so superior that you would think you had no competition, and you would dawdle away the development of your superiorities. And then you would be surpassed by those who made **PAD** a point of emphasis in their lives, but who lacked the positive benefits of **TAG**. Teresa M. Amabile of Harvard University, writing in *The American Psychologist*, April 2001, says "although lay people and creativity theorists often make the assumption that creativity depends primarily on talent, there is considerable evidence **that hard work and intrinsic motivation . . . play central roles.**" (Underlining is ours.)

So **PON** (Press On Now) **with PAD** (Persistence And Determination) **in attacking each day's tasks.** Pay careful attention to gaining the objective of each action, so that you form a well-ingrained *habit of setting up* **PON** *unconsciously and automatically* whenever you start a new set of actions in handling a new problem. Temper it all with *common sense* in knowing when and where and how to persist on a point or to slack off for a time. Determination is not lost if you *over-arch* the problem with it, and see where the overall scene can best be determined while maintaining periods or points of relaxation and pleasure.

We will lead you to practice all of this in the exercises of our **Method** of analyzing your values and clearing up any malfunctioning mechanisms of escape and defense. Then we will guide you toward the purposive behavior that can effectively handle underlying difficulties. We will do this through showing you how to apply each action in the *Method* by a *programmed development of habits* that will stick with you in attacking all future problems and conflicts.

Several illustrative cases will show how it works in everyday life. Of course you won't see in them the **formalized** actions which we have presented. The latter are merely to help you practice in duplicating—with greater effectiveness—what these individuals have either chanced upon or gained through a rather helter-skelter trial and error process which has taken them much more time than you will have to spend when you use our formal practice techniques. When these actions become an unconscious habit you will no longer have even to think of them; they will have become "second nature" to you.

Before giving these cases, however, we must call your attention to a serious caveat (or warning). This applies to everyone who selects any meaning and purpose in life: When

you choose a goal you must be aware of all of its contingencies and be willing to accept responsibility for them.

This means we must **precede PON** with **FATE** (First Attend the Effects). You will see what we mean when you read the first case.

Several Cardinal Examples of PON with PAD

Case No. 1: An Example of PON with PAD in Politics. This case is that of a young man who wanted to be an artist (oil painter) although he had absolutely no talent. At age 23 he was very sad and depressed, and felt his future was hopeless. From childhood on he was unkempt and had no interest in women, although he was not a homosexual. He was **apparently** simply asexual. But his behavior showed the marks of profound sexual repression; sex was "displaced" by attention to injustices which angered him. Years later he acquired a mistress who really loved him, but he would alternate between attempts at commitment and phobic withdrawal. He had, however, one driving feeling that in spite of his earlier hopelessness he was supposed to achieve something great. He failed miserably at visual art and architecture. He hated manual labor, but at times he was forced to do it in order to survive. He lived from soup kitchen to soup kitchen, from flop house to flop house, amid their roaches, filth, decay, and infestation. Deeply resenting the political and economic conditions around him, he began to be a "stump talker", and found that he could easily interest other malcontents.

Gradually he learned what it took to achieve political power. One factor was not to antagonize the dominant institutions, including those of religion in the area. He was extremely right winged in thinking but he knew where to back off. He did succeed in gaining leadership of a small party, of which he had used his considerable talent at oratory to gain control. He had failed to recognize this one talent in his earlier life struggles. Now he began to see it, however, and gradually he became a dominant political figure in the country. It is all based on **PON** with **PAD** which, when practiced leads to the self-confidence and self-esteem that is the key to success. Of course he never heard of this phrase *per se*, but he discovered the same principle on his own.

This man who started so humbly manipulated his small political following to eventual success beyond his wildest earlier dreams; and he eventually became a broad based political power known to all in his generation. His opponents eventually won out, but only after a long and bitter struggle. His eventual defeat did not lessen the degree of success which he maintained for some years.

Can you guess who this political figure was? We might preface the question by adding the information that he was eventually rejected not only by his party but also by the world. Thus the gaining of a passionate political arm as well as a powerful influence in the world of his time did not portend a "good" life for a socially beneficial power—as a matter of fact it was actually just the opposite.

This creates the *caveat* which we noted in searching for a life meaning and for subsequent purposive acts to fulfill the meaning: We must evaluate the social, political, economic, cultural, moral and ethical consequences or contingencies of our purposive goals. If we maintain awareness of these factors we will then have either to modify our choices to conform to socially approved contingencies or to accept full responsibility for the effect of these choices.

The man in our illustrative case had failed to do either. Thus he was destroyed, and even his memory became a pariah to his own people.

His name? Now the question will seem easier as we answer: Adolph Hitler.

So—**PON** with **PAD** but **FATE! (First Attend the Effects!)**

Case No. 2: An Example from Religion. A young preacher, associate pastor in a large southern city church, was unable to accept the *status quo* because of the great injustices in it. He became a religious activist, but was put down time and again by the more powerful forces in this environment. He persisted with determination against all odds, and became an outstanding orator. Resisting the violence all around him, he persisted against all personal danger. His opponents gave rise to one out-of-control hothead who assassinated the young preacher, and thereby enabled him to accomplish on a grand scale more reform in death than he could ever have achieved in life. By **PON** with **PAD** he had raised his cause to greater heights than any amount of talent and genius alone could have produced.

His name? Martin Luther King, Jr.

Case No. 3: An Example from Music. About 1790 a young man left home to study music in Vienna. At first he worked under the famous Franz Joseph Haydn, who was unimpressed by the student. Then the young man switched to another great teacher, Johann Albrechtsberger, who later said of him, "That man never learned anything, and he will never write any worthwhile music." But the student kept to the **PON** with **PAD** which had driven him over the years. In the long run this paid off.

The young man's name: Ludwig van Beethoven.

Case No. 4: An Example from Science. A fifteen-year old boy was dismissed from his school in Munich because of lack of interest in his studies. While reports have persisted that he was considered to be retarded, he actually did well in subjects that interested him. But because of lack of interest he failed the test to enter a polytechnics school and failed as a tutor, and was rejected as a teaching assistant. Finally through family contacts he got a job in a Bern patent office. He drifted along over some years. But behind the scenes he had paid powerful attention to

PON with **PAD** with which he had pursued his true life interest, mathematics. Yes he had **TAG**, but without the **PON** with **PAD** he never would have been recognized.

His name? Albert Einstein.

PON With PAD Always Applies to Situations of Conflict

Just as a play, novel or short story has no appeal without some sort of conflict or contest or competition or game quality, so life is boring and without meaning (the state of "existential vacuum" or empty existence described by the late Dr. Viktor Frankl of the University of Vienna Medical School) without a challenge to overcome obstacles. But the contest must be fair and winnable. Conflicts with spouse, siblings, parents, children, sports adversaries, business or professional competitors—all must have a way of resolution or reduction. In story form the contest ends with the leading characters "living happily ever after" and the villains being badly beaten. In real life it isn't that simple, but you will be able, by the method we are teaching you, to approach this ideal in resolving most of your conflicts.

As you examine these conflicts carefully you will see that what we have been saying about a factor of meaningful intimacy in each and every conflict is really true. To find evidence of this all you have to do is to look at movies, TV, plays, novels, sports, casinos, music, and so forth. And of course it will be apparent in most relationships in business offices and industrial concerns, in most clubs, even church functions. As you reflect upon it all you will see that when they say, **"sex is what makes the world go 'round!"**, *this is true, but behind it all except the most pornographic sex is a yearning for a meaningful intimacy with another person. Unfortunately the entertainment industry in America has produced so much "sex for its own sake" that foreign cultures get the impression that "raw" sex is all that Americans think about. Hopefully this is* **not** *true of the "Silent Majority" (no implied relation to Dr. Jerry Falwell), the people with moderately conservative sexual attitudes and behavior, but who do* not resist the entertainment claims of "American freedom" from all restrictions under their interpretation of the First Amendment.

In terms of the **PON** with **PAD** mechanism everyday conflicts (Frankl's "Meanings of the Moment") can best be approached through our stage by stage procedure, starting with the slightest momentary success and building on it to the point of successful attainment of a very simple goal which you have selected in accordance with the procedure.

Our case studies have shown some real life examples of how this works. It will work for you also, if you organize your efforts through the procedures which we have presented. In the following work you will be guided by reminders of the **PON** with **PAD** mechanism. There will be some sections (such as the demographic or personal history blanks to point up your present basic circumstance) in which the procedure would not be called for. And some items in a given exercise may also not involve this procedure. These will be made clear as the text proceeds.

You are now prepared to enter the chapters which give the steps in our method of finding your deepest and most satisfying meanings. When you complete them you will have achieved the full effects of:

PON with PAD!

To make it all easier see the **Abstract** on the next page.

ABSTRACT
of
The PON (PRESS ON NOW) with PAD (PERSISTENCE AND DETERMINATION) Method of MOTIVATION

SUMMARY OF PROCEDURES FOR SUCCESS:

Choose Immediate Goal, either from assigned exercises or from personal immediate life situations. In the latter case,

Evaluate the goal by FATE:

FATE: (First Attend The Effects) Are the effects or consequences or contingencies of attaining this goal those for which you are willing to accept responsibility? If not, choose a different goal. If so, FATE is good to you and leads to persistence.

Xerograph the PRESS ON logo below, cut it out and paste it sideways on one side of a 3x5 card.

> **PRESS ON**
>
> NOTHING IN THE WORLD CAN TAKE THE PLACE OF PERSISTENCE TALENT WILL NOT; NOTHING IS MORE COMMON THAN UNSUCCESSFUL PEOPLE WITH TALENT. GENIUS WILL NOT; UNREWARDED GENIUS IS ALMOST A PROVERB. EDUCATION WILL NOT; THE WORLD IS FULL OF EDUCATED DERELICTS. PERSISTENCE AND DETERMINATION ALONE ARE ALL POWERFUL.

Now PON with PAD and see how easy it is to begin to succeed—and then to build the habits of success in daily life!

And now you will be ready to begin conquest of the **SEVEN STEPS TO A NEW MISSION AND MEANING IN LIFE.**

Chapter III

Step I

Discovering Who You Really Are

WELCOME TO THE program which can help you become what you want to be—and drop out what you want not to be—in fulfillment of your life goals. To begin this you need first to look at where you now stand in life, and to compare this with where you really want to stand. Together we will evaluate the differences. Then we will analyze the factors which block your achievement, and the requirements to remove the blockage. And then we will examine your life history for the hidden assets which can, in spite of all handicaps, failures and set-backs, lead you to success. Yes, whether or not you believe it now, we can discover such assets. Together we can and will find them, because they really are there for the people who are willing to take the time and put out the energy necessary to discover them.

> "Full many a gem of purest ray serene
> The dark unfathomed caves of ocean bear;
> Full many a flower is born to blush unseen
> And waste its fragrance on the desert air."
> —Grey's *Elegy Written In A Country Churchyard*.

Stick with us and we'll show you how to discover these hidden assets. But before you can discover the meaning of your life and the goals to fulfill them you must have clearly in mind the *values* underlying them—the personal values for which you would sacrifice greatly if necessary, the values which can make life worth facing all of its problems.

Now through the rest of Chapter III Step 1 we will hardly be mentioning gender. This is because what you will do in the exercises of Step 1 is independent of your own gender, and we don't want you to get snagged by thinking of your own values as typical of either gender: They are not tied to gender, though you may conclude **after** determining them for yourself that some specific values are **for your own analysis** different between genders.

After we complete these exercises and you have a clear picture of your own values, you will then find that as you employ these values you will—as when you do anything else—see that there is a gender aspect **in their application**. But for the present forget about gender as you complete Step 1.

An excellent exercise to start is The Identity Exercise (Exercise No. 1). Do it now. (p. 158)

—O—

And now that you've done No.1, the next exercise will help you to pinpoint just what you really do value in life. It is The Role Model Exercise (Exercise No. 2). Do it as soon as you have finished No. 1. (p.162)

—O—

Having done Exercises 1 and 2, you have no doubt begun to see a pattern in your life experiences and the values which have grown from them. But yet another exercise is needed now to firm up these values and to reveal the kind of goals which will fulfill them.

This is the MILE (Meaning in Life Evaluation) form, Exercise 3. So do this one now. (p. 165)

—O—

And now that you have completed the three exercises of Chapter III, you should have a pretty good picture of where you are and where you want to go in life. But we have still one more important question (not cast in the form of an exercise this time, but rather in thought as you read on before entering Step 2). In the systematic exploration of just what blend of values is best for *you*, you need to determine where you want to stand on the value spectrum from the mechanistic, materialistic and purely objective world to the teleological (purposive), intuitive, subjective and *noetic* (spiritual—though not *necessarily* religious) world.

Choosing Your View of Life

Throughout the entire recorded history of the human race there have been two—and only two—basic attitudes of human beings toward themselves. We find these in ancient Egyptian cultures, in Hebrew life at the time of Christ, and in the America of the last part of the twentieth century. And after five thousand years of recorded history, there is no accurate way of settling the issue of which one is correct, there is no more proof of the validity of either than there was in the beginning. So you have to make your own evaluation and choose the view that seems most reasonable to you.

Herein you will find few references to sex. But sex enters in the same ways as in all other human relationships; you have already learned these ways, and we will not emphasize them further in this chapter, because we now want you to concentrate on the non-sexual aspects of this choice.

Which you choose does make an important difference,

because your choice will determine *how* you are going to proceed in the search for life meaning. And it is important that you do make a choice and not try to evade the question, for those who take the latter course—and they include a large segment of the human race—never really find a true meaning and purpose in life. This is because any genuine meaning stems from one or the other of the two views.

1. Humankind is merely a machine, a mechanical device; his biological organism follows the mechanical laws of nature as do all other aspects of nature, and he is nothing more than any other organism—such as a rat or a cat—except that he is more complex. All of nature is the result of chance factors; in spite of the regularities of natural laws, there is no purpose and meaning behind it. Of course this view would logically hold that there is no afterlife or survival of personality after death.

This is the view of so-called positivistic science, the view of "mechanism," the "reductionist" view which holds that all of man's psychological processes can be reduced to physical processes, the view of "determinism," which considers all mental and physical events to be caused or determined by physical antecedents.

This mechanistic view says that there is no **intrinsic** meaning or purpose in life. Man's only chance for meaningful living is based on what he can devise for himself. He must lift himself by his own bootstraps, because there is no external help for him from any "Higher Power." Some, including the famous Harvard behaviorist psychologist, the late B. F. Skinner, would even deny that humanity can do anything for itself, since they believe life is entirely determined by external forces. They believe that if all people would choose to become conditioned as Skinner specified there could be a great future, but that because most people have been conditioned by their environment not to accept his conditioning they cannot accept it by "free will" because the Skinner people believe there is no free will. So all is hopeless in the end.

The mechanistic view of man is in many respects illustrated by the philosophy of the famous French existentialist Jean-Paul Sartre. Sartre was the leader of atheistic existentialism. Existentialism, which also has a theistic branch, holds that the focus of the study of humankind should be on its existence as a human being. And both branches hold that human life cannot be understood by reason alone, and that man has freedom of choice as to how he will face life.

But Sartre believed that there is no meaning and purpose in the universe other than what each human individual can put there for himself. All life is *absurd* (a technical term in existentialism that means, not that life is ridiculous, but that it cannot be comprehended by reason). We are all doomed to defeat in the end, according to Sartre, for there is no justice in nature. But in spite of this, we can each find some values in which we believe, and we can live by these values to the last. And living thus—superimposing our own meanings on a meaningless world—enables us to be superior to the absurdity of it all and to die with dignity in the knowledge that we created our own meaning where there really is none. All of this makes life worth living, as Sartre sees it.

Yes, this is the world of the late Jean-Paul Sartre, and positive scientists such as Skinner have a similar view, although they differ on such matters as freedom of the will. As we have said, they deny the existence of freedom. And this is the world of most behavioral scientists today, especially most psychologists. The majority of psychologists consider themselves behaviorists, holding that only behavior, and not subjective experience (or conscious experience), is admissible "evidence" in the study of man because this kind of evidence cannot be measured physically. The present first writer, a psychologist, strongly disagrees.

There is another view, which also has always been with us:

2. Human beings are machines, but they are also infinitely more than machines. Their psychological processes, conscious experience, emotions, and feelings do involve processes in the brain and in the rest of the nervous system and the body, but they cannot **all** be **reduced** to bodily processes and measured by presently known scientific methods. This snag of **reductionism** (in psychology it is called the psycho-physical axiom) has long been a thorn in the side of scientists who are also religious: It has seemed to them that it knocks out any possibility of spiritual phenomena. But the work of mathematical physicist Frank Tipler demonstrates that all psychological processes really have a physical basis. It is our incomplete knowledge of physical laws that makes them **seem** "supernatural." Tipler believes in immortality and demonstrates how it can be accomplished physically. (See Tipler, Frank. **The Physics of Immortality**, New York: Anchor Books. Doubleday, 1994.) Failure to recognize Tipler's point has probably done more than anything else to cause people who would like to reject the mechanistic view of life to be in conflict between the two while usually supporting mechanism because it is "scientific." Tipler shows that this division is apparent but not real, and that in reality there is no conflict between true science and true religion.

People are more than a biological organism—they are unique beings set apart in nature from all other beings. As the philosopher Max Scheler has noted, people have one capacity not shared by any other of the creatures of Earth: the capacity to contemplate the possible. Only humankind can see, not merely what is, but what can and should be. The dog accepts nature as is and has no concept of a better world, but people can conceive of a whole new way of life and can work toward its attainment. They are not limited by the past or even the present; they can control their future.

This view holds that the universe is not merely the product of chance but is designed by a Higher Intelligence greater than that of humanity. It considers people as a part of this design and therefore believes that they have their own unique meaning and purpose.

And if this is true of Homo sapiens as a species, it is also true of each man and woman as an individual. We all have a destiny to fulfill, a life purpose to carry out.

Each of us must search for it; when we become convinced that we have discovered it we have a real mission to fulfill, a cause to work for, a task to complete in life that will motivate us to such a powerful degree that we can go on. We will continue in spite of life's frustrations and make it through or over or under or around obstacles because we have a reason that makes it all worth the struggle.

This view would logically hold that there is some sort of afterlife or persistence of personality after bodily death, although there are those who embrace the view without believing in survival. This nonmechanistic orientation rejects determinism and holds that we are all free within the limits set by heredity and environment to choose how we will face our situation. As Frankl says, life conditions are given to us; how we face them is freely chosen by us.

This is the world of the religious person, but it is also the world of many who do not think of themselves as religious—of many who would certainly not be religious in the institutional sense, in the sense of organized religion, in the "church" sense, but who do believe in a Power greater than man, and who have their own personal ways of contacting this Power. Alcoholics Anonymous is based on this approach, in which each individual defines his own concept of this Power but still turns to it for help.

This is the world of those who believe that there is a Power toward which every person can turn for help, whether he does it by religion in the conventional sense or by his own methods. It is a world of purpose and design in which each individual life counts, in which we make our lives count in spite of whatever setbacks and tragedies and frustrations we face. We do this by looking for the hidden meaning in it all, for the way in which all of our life events fit into a pattern and point to a purpose we can fulfill, to a meaning we would not have been able to realize if these problems had not occurred.

This is the *attitudinal value* in logotherapy, described by Frankl. The attitudinal value can be applied by those who follow the mechanistic view of man, by their asking themselves what they can do to turn their rotten luck into some advantage; but it is much more easily applied by nonmechanistic believers in an intrinsic purpose in all of nature, for they do not have to consider their conditions as "rotten luck." They rather think of these conditions as part of a purpose that is to be discovered and fulfilled.

This second, nonmechanistic view is called the "teleological" view by philosophers (from the Greek *teleos*, "aim, goal or end"), for it holds that there is a plan or design in nature toward which natural events are moving. For most people this view is not only a more optimistic attitude toward life, but also a helpful and needed source of courage when the going in life gets tough. **Most people's teeth are not sharp enough and their fingernails are not long enough to go it alone** in the human jungle that they often find themselves facing. But for some, such as Jean-Paul Sartre and psychologist-sexologist Albert Ellis, this attitude represents a failure of the individual to take responsibility for life upon his own shoulders and to handle this situation without "magical" help (which these authorities believe does not exist in the first place, and which they say they do not want in the second place).

Well, which of the two views of humankind is right? As we

have said, the truth is that leading spokesmen for both points of views agree that neither view can be proven in the scientific sense. Both are in the last analysis a matter of faith. Many religious persons have a deep and abiding faith that there is a Creator who has a specific plan for their lives. Many people such as Sartre have a faith that there is not. **Sartre said that he intuitively knew there is no God, just as Billy Graham would say that he intuitively knows there is one.**

All of this leads many to try to avoid the issue altogether until they reach some life crisis when they need to come to grips with it and to have a faith upon which they can base action. The trouble with such procrastination is that, if you wait until you need a faith, you won't be able to establish it overnight. Whichever way your faith may turn, it has to jell and become a genuine part of you. And until you have a firm decision that fits your personal needs, you won't have real peace of mind. You can settle for the intermediate view if you wish, as multitudes do. But it is very dangerous in facing the future which is unknown to all of us.

People are emotionally different in their needs to believe in these two views. You will be able to find a real meaning and purpose in life from either view *if* (1) you *really* believe in it, and (2) you are *emotionally suited* to believe in and to accept this view. The latter factor hangs many people up today. They are trying in this increasingly secular society to believe in, or to live as if they believed in, the mechanistic view that there is no purposeful design in the universe placed there by some Creator. They consider the teleological view mystical, supernatural, and fairy-tale-like, and they want no part of it—until they meet a life situation in which they discover that they are not the superstrong stainless steel independent types they thought they were, and that they really do need some help. Then it is too late to get the help, because their doubts of a purposeful universe have become so firmly ingrained that they cannot readily over-arch their previous perceptions in favor of new (to them) and meaningful teleological terms. If the factors dictating the need to change persist, these people usually make it in the long run, but this period of "no-man's-land" will be unpleasant and dangerous to their well-being.

The point is well illustrated by a patient the first writer had in one of his logotherapy groups in an alcoholic rehabilitation program some years ago. Believe it or not, he was a large-city psychiatrist. When we came to study the present topic, he was deeply moved..

"Doctor," he said, "I am here in the hospital because I cannot resolve this problem in my own mind. I know that's why I drink. I have the emotional need to believe that there is a meaning and purpose in the universe, put there by a Creator who cares about me and will help me fulfill that purpose if I turn to him and seek to find it. But when I try, I am beset with doubts, and I can't stick to either view. I tolerate it as long as I can, and then I grab a bottle."

"Doctor," I returned, "you are not alone in this struggle. There is no proof, but there *is* a lot of evidence. There is evidence on both sides, and each side is convincing to many people who are suited for it. If you will really take the time and energy to search for the evidence on the side you need to believe in, you will find it. And only then will you find yourself."

He went through a long struggle that discouraged him, and he left the hospital without finding himself. But within a year, he had come to grips with the question well enough to get back into practice. When he finds others fighting this battle, he will know how they feel and will probably be better able to help than would a psychiatrist to whom the problem has no personal significance.

For those like him who need to believe in a Higher Power but haven't found satisfactory evidence, the following facts may help:

1. Scientists are losing a degree of their sense of intellectual superiority, according to Richard Olson of the University of

California at Santa Cruz, writing in *Psychology Today*, January 1976. He notes that certain developments within the sciences, such as the Heisenberg Indeterminacy or Uncertainty Principle, have indicated that there are some physical events that cannot be predicted by natural laws.

2. Elizabeth Kübler-Ross, M.D., whose book *On Death and Dying* (1969) is perhaps the best-known work concerning the terminally ill, has for many years been collecting reports of a large number of individuals who were pronounced medically dead but who later were resuscitated, and who retained memories of this period during which they were supposedly dead. *Reader's Digest* (August 1976) reports interviews with Dr. Kübler-Ross for *Family Circle* and *People* magazines, in which she talked of her conclusions from her studies. She had before then doubted there is any life after death, but changed her mind firmly afterward. She feels that something significant happens within minutes after "clinical" death, as her patients became amazingly peaceful in expression at that time.

Kübler-Ross investigated scores of patients, both religious and non-religious, some of whom had been "dead" for three to twelve hours. Most reported one basic type of experience: they felt as if they had shed their physical bodies, and they experienced peace, freedom from pain and anxiety, and a sense of completeness or perfection. Some could "see" the efforts to revive them, and they resented attempts to return them to a life of suffering. None was afraid to die again. A common characteristic of their experiences was their ineffability—there were no adequate words to describe it.

In February 1977, it was the first writer's privilege to participate in a Festival of Meaning honoring Dr. Viktor Frankl, the founder of logotherapy, organized by Dr. Robert Leslie of the Pacific School of Religion in Berkeley, California, upon the occasion of the establishment there of the Frankl Library and Memorabilia. At a dinner for Dr. Frankl, the famous Viennese psychiatrist mentioned that Dr. Kübler-Ross had recently come to see him. I asked him how he had reacted to her collection of cases. He pointed out that, because the concepts of time and space are human psychological constructs and have meaning only in the world of human experience, it is really not valid to think in terms of events after death or before life. This means that, in a sense apart from the human experience of the sequence of events which we consider as time and of the distances which we know as space, the concepts of past, present and future blend, and the meanings of "here" versus "there" merge. Thus life becomes a continuous process (even though it changes in form of expression) without beginning or end. Following the evidence produced by Kübler-Ross, and the remainder of the relative nature of the time-space continua noted by Frankl, one might conclude that it is a basic human mistake to interpret birth-life-death sequences in terms of beginning and end; they are rather episodes that transcend time and space. Frankl held that no experience, once it occurs, can ever be lost—it remains always as an occurrence in nature regardless of all other events that may transpire. (See Frankl's book, *The Unheard Cry for Meaning: Psychotherapy and Humanism*. New York: Simon and Schuster, 1978; specifically the chapter, "Temporality and Mortality.")

The sum of these facts suggests that life cannot be adequately viewed as an accidental flash in a meaningless universe of absurdity and chaos, but that it is part of a continuing, dynamic, unfolding process. And how can such a process, which is by definition *not* "chance determined" and chaotic, occur without some kind of Power or Intelligence in the universe to determine or ordain it?

As Martin Heidegger, the late great German existentialist philosopher, said, "The *existential question* [the question of the meaning of existence] is not, Why is this or that here? The real existential question is, Why is there something instead of nothing at all?"

Winston Churchill said to the United States Congress on December 26, 1941, shortly after America's entry into World War II, "I will say that any man must have a blind soul who cannot see that some great purpose and design is being worked out here below." Eugene A. Cernan, Apollo 17 astronaut, said (*The Plain Truth*, June 1976), "When you get out there a quarter of a million miles from home, you look at Earth with a little different perspective.... The Earth looks so perfect. There are no strings to hold it up.... You think of the infinity of space and time. I didn't see God but I am convinced of God by the order out in space. I know it didn't happen by accident."

3. The biggest barrier to belief in a Higher Power for many is the sense of thwarted justice that seems to pervade human life. If there were a Higher Power, why would He (or It—or She, in deference to Women's Lib) permit such horrendous circumstances to occur? And when they occur to us, our natural first reaction is, Why me? The answer to this question is crucial in our capacity to find any real meaning and purpose in our lives.

Those whose answer is, It is my rotten luck—the result of "pure chance" in a meaningless universe—must then, in order to find any personal life meaning in this meaningless world, ask themselves the further questions: What can I do on my own, lifting myself by my own bootstraps, since there is no external help, to turn my misfortunes to my own advantage? How can I use them constructively to create a meaning where none now seems to exist in nature? Persons who reason thus must accept responsibility to create such a meaning or perish in despair.

On the other hand, those whose answer to the first question is, These misfortunes and injustices do not seem to make any sense, but I accept them as a part of a plan or design in nature, as a part of the design for my own life, as having a purpose that I cannot see, even though it appears so horribly unjust—those whose answer is along these lines must next ask themselves, a second question, What could this purpose be?

Now their third question will be the same as that of those who believe the universe is meaningless and the result of pure chance: What can I now do to use my misfortunes constructively, to turn my suffering to advantage by finding something worthwhile to do that I could not have done so well if these tragedies had not occurred? You may wonder, therefore, what difference it makes whether we believe the universe is chaotic or designed. But there is a big difference here: The "design people" don't have to say, What rotten breaks, but I'll lift myself by my own bootstraps and go on anyway, even though it is very hard to keep up courage in such a terrible world. They instead say, My experiences have been terrible, but they have a purpose that I am supposed to fulfill. Therefore I will search for this purpose, I will try to see what these experiences could be intended to teach me or in what direction they could be leading me. I will choose the positive attitude that such purpose exists, and I will search for it. And in the search I can expect help: I do not have to depend solely on my own strength in a world that is too much for any man; I can look to this Higher Power that has ordained the purpose I cannot see, and I can expect guidance in the search and assistance when I falter. Of course I still may never in this life understand the purpose; it may always seem unjust to me. But I will know that purpose is there, and in the afterlife it will be understandable.

A strong point regarding this matter of dealing with a frustrated sense of justice in an unjust world is often made by Viktor Frankl: he asks, "Do you suppose that an animal in a laboratory experiment can understand the meaning of its suffering?" Can it comprehend the fact that this unpleasantness serves a purpose higher than any that its limitations permit it to grasp? In the same way, is it not possible that man experiences suffering that has a purpose higher than any that his own limitations permit him to see?

In this connection, an incident in the first writer's own experience may illustrate what Frankl is talking about as he deals with this difficulty which most people have in maintaining faith and courage in the face of the ubiquitous occurrence of grossly unjust and unexpected human suffering. One evening the writer attended church where the preacher's homily included the statement that, when he was in seminary, his brother, who was also expecting to become a minister, drowned. His first reaction to the tragedy was to withdraw from seminary. Why should he serve such an unjust God? Fortunately his mother's influence in facing the situation with courage and faith finally turned his own tide and enabled him to go on.

As the writer returned home with this sermon in mind, he had to step over a freshly painted doorstep to enter his condominium. The next-door neighbor was outside, and the writer was suddenly greeted by her dog, which he had often petted. But now he had to halt the dog's advance upon the fresh paint by a sharp rejecting attitude. The neighbor, seeing what was happening, cuffed the dog sharply, and he yelped in retreat.

The author wondered how the dog would react when the animal next saw him, how he would make sense of the fact that this man petted him one day and the next rejected him for no apparent reason, and then after that attempted to pet him again. How do you explain to a dog that it was necessary to hurt him in order to prevent greater injury (in this case, getting his paws full of poisonous lead paint, which he undoubtedly would have tried to lick off; as well as his unknowingly injuring others through ruining the paint job)?

How do you explain to a dog the reason for events that are beyond his world of experience and therefore his comprehension? How does God explain to a person?

No, the dog didn't understand; but when I next saw him, he wagged his tail in friendship. He had accepted me on faith, based on the good experiences of the past and in spite of the bad. He wasn't bitter about what he couldn't comprehend. Sometimes dogs are smarter than people.

4. The questions of whether the universe is designed and purposeful and of whether there is a Higher Power that made it so are closely related, as we have seen, to the question of personal survival after death. The latter issue may be better understood

by consideration of the fact that personal survival *before* death does not actually occur. That is to say, we do not maintain the same identity throughout life, even though there is a degree of continuity. This concept is well known in the metamorphosis of some insects, wherein, for example, a caterpillar changes into a moth; but we usually do not associate such a process with human life. And yet in the human organism an analogous process does take place. As we grow from infancy to childhood to adulthood to old age, we go through both physical and mental stages between which there is a thread of continuity based on remembered experience and habits of behavior, but which are separated by differences in appearance, thinking, and behavior that are really more distinct from each other than the differences between many individuals at a given period of life. If you are over forty, you are in many respects more like your contemporary friends than you are like yourself at the age of eight.

Thus we do not survive this life unchanged; we do not really survive as the same person. We can therefore hardly expect to survive the transition of death unchanged, though the latter may be seen as a *sudden* transition in comparison with the *slow* transition from youth to old age. But here again, since time and space are concepts based on the experience of this life, experience apart from it may not reflect this same sense of time difference. Survival may therefore occur without involving the rigid continuation of form and matter in the frame of reference of time and space to which we are accustomed. And this survival may be based on purpose and design in a meaningful universe, in which we can look to a Higher Power for guidance and help.

Evidence that the universe is not a mere mechanism as conceived by materialistic science, but that there are "nonmechanistic" laws yet unknown in nature (which open the door for the concepts of design and purpose in the universe, and for the existence of a Higher Intelligence) is abundant in the field of *parapsychology*. Formerly called psychic phenomena, the occurrences studied in this field include psycho-kinesis ("mind-over-matter" manifestations), appearances and disappearances that seem to defy the known laws of natural science, mental telepathy and clairvoyance (named ESP or extrasensory perception by Dr. J. B. Rhine at Duke University), and various other related effects.

They are now known as *psi* phenomena. Although many skeptics still exist, the study of these phenomena has considerable scientific acceptance today, as witnessed by the fact that there is a division of parapsychology in the American Association for the Advancement of Science, whereas parapsychologists could not have gotten through the *back* door of this august body a generation ago.

It is true that the parapsychologists (so called because the "orthodox" psychologists considered them outside of respectable psychology in the early years: Greek *para* means beyond, outside) have not yet produced a truly "repeatable" laboratory experiment. This means one that can be duplicated in virtually any scientific laboratory at will with essentially the same results; and the first writer personally holds out for this criterion as essential, because it has been a cornerstone of proof in all *experimental* sciences. But the evidence for psi phenomena has continually grown stronger over the last forty years.

There is voluminous literature on the subject, which you may find at any good library. The laboratory work is essential to proof, but it grows out of the vast background of frequently reported human experiences that seem to involve such phenomena. We will give only two examples here, since you can find an abundance of them in the literature. In fact, you very well may have some such experience to add yourself; and if you do not, the chances are excellent that someone close to you does have.

A lady told this story:

"The strangest event of my life occurred on one evening in February. I kept saying that it was not my voice, and yet it had to be. There was no one else around except my escort, who was standing just behind me, ready to open the car door. 'Did you say that?' he asked. 'Did you say, "Don't go down Averill Street"? It didn't sound like you.' 'I—I don't know—it wasn't my voice,' I faltered.

"Actually Averill Street was the closest route to my home from the supper club where we had just finished a quiet meal. At the time I had just begun to recover from a very serious illness and had not been out of the house for two months. My friends had all tried to help in the recovery, and Sam, my escort, whom I had known only as a good friend of my late husband's, took me out for an evening of 'real food and fine music for a change.'

"I had gone against my better judgment, because I had felt apprehensive for no apparent reason. As we now pulled out of the parking lot, Sam said, 'Teresa, I see no reason why we can't go down Averill Street. Do you know of any reason why we shouldn't?' 'No,' I replied, 'I don't know why I said that. It's not my nature to back-seat drive. It just didn't seem like I said it, but I must have. No, Sam, of course there is no reason why we can't go down Averill Street.'

"So we went down Averill. And only several minutes later we were hit broadside on my side of the car by another automobile. Our car was totaled, and I suffered a crushed side and permanent nerve damage to my right arm. Sam was not injured.

"When he was allowed to see me in the hospital, his first words were, 'How in the hell did you know we should not have gone down Averill Street?' 'I don't know,' I managed to mumble. 'It just wasn't my voice. And don't blame yourself, because I was warned, and I disregarded the warning.' Even today, on the occasions when my right arm gives me fits, I think back to that strange occurrence and wonder what really happened."

What do you think happened?

The same lady very recently told another story:

"The air was cold and damp this morning, and I wore a head scarf as I drove alone to church, even though head gear is seldom necessary here on the Gulf Coast. As I approached to within two blocks of the church, it felt as though someone in the back seat behind me had suddenly plucked the scarf off of my head. I looked around as best I could while driving, and of course there was no one else in the car, and I could not see the scarf. All of the doors and windows were tightly closed because of the cold weather.

"When I parked the car I began to search for the scarf, but it was nowhere to be found. Thinking it might fall out as I opened the door, I watched closely, and then I searched all around the car and thoroughly in the back, under the seats, and everywhere, but nothing!"

The following morning the lady had her husband vacuum the car and make a thorough search, but nothing was found.

"I simply couldn't believe it," she said, "but my sense of humor finally came through, and I said to myself, 'If I'd known the spooks needed a scarf so badly, I'd have worn a brand new one, and not my old favorite.'"

Well, what do you think happened in this case? Is the lady lying? Are these events hoaxes? Coincidences? Hallucinations? Is the lady crazy?

I don't think so. You will understand why when I tell you that she has never shown any interest in parapsychology, spiritualism, mysticism, or any form of the occult. She is a devout believer in institutional religion, and she has always accepted the existence of a world beyond man's understanding on the basis of a firm but uncomplicated faith, without attempts to rationalize it or to probe its nature. She has never been known to center her thoughts on manifestations of the nonmaterial world, because she has never needed these to bolster her faith.

These manifestations are very abundant in the literature of parapsychology. Now if you are a hard-core mechanist, you will assume such things are impossible, and that people who report them must be lying, crazy, self-deceived, the victims of hoax or coincidence. If you have already determined not to believe, no amount of evidence—not even that of your own eyes—will convince you. But if you have an open mind, you will do a lot of wondering about reports of this type.

And you may find in parapsychology what you need as a basis for a reasonable faith that there is more to the universe than mechanistic science allows. Here you may gain encouraging evidence that there is, after all, some sort of purpose and design in nature and that back of it exists a designing Power.

6. In conceiving the question of design in the universe, it may help to draw an analogy between what you have to do in interpreting this universe and what you do in perceiving the ambiguous stimuli provided by "projective techniques" in clinical psychology. The best known of these techniques is the Rorschach Ink Blot Test, a series of ten supposedly meaningless ink blots which are variously seen by different people as everything and as nothing under the canopy of heaven. Your personal interpretation will depend upon your unique background of individual experience, although there are common patterns or "popular responses."

Now are these blots the result of "pure chance" or of purpose and design? From one standpoint, they are pure chance, since they were made by pouring ink upon paper with a middle crease and then folding the paper upon the crease and thus smearing the ink. But on the other hand, Hermann Rorschach, the Swiss psychiatrist who invented them, made some ten thousand blots before he got a final ten that elicit the maximal number and variety of responses which he wanted. So from another standpoint, the blots represent an element of purpose and design superimposed upon the pure chance factors that shaped them.

The late great philosopher Alfred North Whitehead believed that something like this occurs in the world of nature: most events are determined by chance; but every so often at key points (which Whitehead called "occasions") in a person's life nonchance factors—the result of purpose and design put there by a Higher Power—do occur.

From this point of view, the universe is sometimes mechanistic and chance determined and sometimes teleological and purposive. To represent a similar kind of comparison, the philosopher Herbert Spencer used an analogy with a curved lens or mirror: from one side it is concave, from the other it is convex. Both interpretations are true, depending upon which side is turned toward us.

From this analogy, it might seem that we could "straddle the fence" by accepting both views of the nature of the world, and thus avoid a choice or decision between them. But here it should be noted that, in order to use the mirror, we must decide the effect we want, and therefore which side we want to move toward to see it. So we really do have to decide what we think about life before we can find a meaning in it.

7. In the last analysis, the strongest line of evidence as to whether there is a Higher Power comes from our individual personal experience. This is always the most convincing argument. Dr. Martial Boudreaux, a psychiatrist whom we shall be quoting presently in connection with evidence for the mechanistic view of the universe, says that he has no religious sentiments, but that the nearest thing to them for him is the moving response he sometimes has to music. This shows that he has correctly identified religion as a personal emotional experience, although he has shut off such experience in his own life.

A psychologist friend who had been religious and then lost her religious faith, said she missed nothing about religion except a sense of Presence—the feeling that someone was always with her, which she had once had. This indicates that religion is not social but personal in essence; and belief in the existence of this sense of Presence or Higher Power is determined, not by reason, but by factors of personal experience, which are primarily related to feelings and emotions.

So the best indicator of what your own position should be on this issue is not your head but your heart. If you have the heart for either of the two views, you will put your head to work in finding supportive evidence for it. And there is plenty for each view, although, as we have said, there is no proof of either.

For the writers the choice has to be a strong commitment to belief in the existence of this Higher Power, and of intrinsic meaning and purpose in a teleological world. The first writer's emotional needs and personal experience in this direction can be shown by an episode in his life some years ago:

Shortly after coming to a new job in a strange community, where he had only a few casual co-worker friends, he had to undergo surgery. The nurse who prepared him for the operation asked, "Who is here with you?"

"What do you mean?"

"Usually when people are operated on, they have a friend or relative who waits outside of the recovery room to see whether or not they make it. Who is waiting for you?"

"Me? Nobody. I've got nobody. I'm here alone."

"Oh.... Well, you'll probably make it okay."

One can feel awfully alone at a time like that. Unless you've been there, you don't know how alone.

While he was being prepared, he had a lot of time to feel that isolation, and it can be frightening. He thought of the others around him with families who cared, and he longed for a comforting hand.

And then it was as if there were an unseen Presence with him, and he remembered that he had forgotten it but it had not forgotten him. Yes, there really was help when you were not strong enough to go it alone.

He had long been a believer in this Power. Though he was never considered a pious person, most have regarded him as religious, and he has thus regarded himself. He has long maintained connections with institutional religion, and regards this as right for him, though he has been aware that it is not for everybody, not even for all who are religious.

Frankl felt that religion will become more personalized and less institutionalized, even though he did not foresee the collapse of institutional religion. He was little concerned with theology per se, but very concerned with the feeling side of religion. And for the writers, institutionalism helps greatly to maintain and nourish religious feelings. For many others, it serves in an opposite way, to destroy the feelings.

So we each must find our own approach to life meaning, and then—if it involves religion—we must find our own best form of expression of this phenomenon.

All of which reflects the point being herein made, that the really convincing evidence of the existence of a Higher Power comes, for those who find it, from within rather than from without: it stems from personal experience.

Now what about the other side of the coin? What lines of evidence are there for those who do not experience a need to believe in this Power, who really show no emotional need for it, and who prefer, like Jean-Paul Sartre, to go through life alone without expecting any outside help? What evidence is there that there is *not* such a Power?

The truth is that, since there is no universal negative, and the existence of such a Power can never be scientifically disproved any more than it can be proved; the negative evidence is, as we have seen, also a matter of faith. But what facts support this kind of faith?

Actually this negative view is based primarily on the assumption that, if there were such a Power, it would be possible to demonstrate the fact scientifically—an assumption that cannot be supported in logic any more than the assumption that the absence of such a Power should be provable scientifically. So one must choose his direction here on the basis of which way his life experience leads him.

This fact is well illustrated through the opinions expressed by a colleague of the first writer, the late Dr. Martial Boudreaux, upon whose ward staff he served as clinical psychologist. He (the writer) distributed a questionnaire aimed at eliciting opinions on both sides of the issue of whether there is intrinsic design and purpose in the universe, and asked respondents to indicate the arguments that were most convincing to them in support of their personal views.

Few would take the time to do the questionnaire; and some who did offered either evidence that had little substance or evidence that was entirely too abstract and complicated to help most people who are searching for answers. But Dr. Boudreaux cut quickly and briefly to the core of the issue; and his views—which are strictly mechanistic and support the position that no Higher Power exists—would serve better than any other material we have come across to represent this orientation. Here is what he said:

> "I opt for the mechanistic or chance viewpoint. The nature of basic physical and chemical organization determines the future over eons of time. How this basic organization came about or if it is universal I have no idea, and could not care less . . . . My evidence is based on the sum total of my experience, and it represents the way I have thought since early youth. It includes the sum total of all of my reading and personal conversations with people of all types. I do not consider either view capable of proof, and I do not find this disconcerting. So you take your choice and go with it. Years ago arguments mattered to me; now I don't care. Both sides are incapable of proof, and both are capable of some refutation . . . . As far as the need for a meaning and purpose in the universe is concerned, I can hack it successfully without one. But each person has to have his own way and to go with it."

There is little that can be added to these statements in representation of the basic mechanistic orientation toward human life. While a large number of people, especially those who are strongly religious on the one hand or strongly antireligious on the other, become quite emotionally biased in their arguments, this psychiatrist maintained an objective attitude toward both views while choosing one attitude for himself. And that is all we can ask of ourselves or of anyone else.

The key to making a personal decision concerning which of these two basic philosophies of life to adopt lies in one's level of personal self-confidence. If you are self-confident, you will trust your ability to make the right decision. Knowing you can't prove either and that the choice must be made on faith, you will—if you lack faith in yourself—also lack faith in your choice. On the other hand, believing in yourself will mean that you will believe in your choice, even though it is made in the face of incomplete data. To have faith in anything, we must first have faith in ourselves.

Actually a large segment of the general population in the United States vacillates between the two views, believing the traditional religious orientation when there is no crisis of need, and drifting thoughtlessly away from it when everything is going well. You are likely to do this unless you take the choice seriously and work at both it and the chapter on self-confidence until you have found a firm answer—the right answer for *you*. When you have done this you will be able to jump from the springboard of values to the position that is right for you, and to maintain this position in the face of life challenges and conflicts. You are now ready for Chapter IV, Step 2, Handling Personal Loss.

Chapter IV

Step 2

Handling Personal Loss

Dealing With Grief, Disappointment,
and the Negative Feelings
Which Block Exploration of Your Life
Situation for New Meanings

NOW THAT YOU have established your real identity in Step 1, you are ready for handling personal loss, grief, and strong emotional upsets in Step 2. First it is important to remember that each step involves relations between the two genders and they are especially significant here.

As you read the various approaches that are now going to be presented for the successful handling of these feelings, keep in mind that although sex may not be mentioned in the several procedures it is always in the background.

Why is this true? Because whenever you have a strong emotional reaction to a loved one, lost permanently or temporarily, you will be dealing either *directly* with a person of the opposite sex, as is the case of a love affair, or *indirectly* through a same-sex person who is associated with the opposite sex of the person for whom you are experiencing the loss. For example, you lose a parent of the same sex but the parent is obviously associated with the parent of the opposite sex. And even if the traumatic association is with a pet, you have unconsciously associated the pet's sex with your own: and, as we have seen, there is always an association (often unconscious) between your experience with your own sex and your experience with the opposite sex.

So no matter how you slice it, the bread of life is bisexual: you have both your own sex and the opposite sex in the equation which will unlock the valves of excruciating tension and enable you to reach a satisfactory adjustment.

The latter does not mean that *all* of the emotional pain will go away. If you have really loved a parent, a child, or a sex partner the scars will never evaporate. But, like the scars of an operation, they will become tolerable and eventually unnoticeable except when some association occurs to bring them up again.

So now let's look at the nitty-gritty of handling such severe and stressful traumas.

Because the basis of grief is so often a failed love affair (married or otherwise), it is important to get in mind what we have called the SEXUAL SATIATION EFFECT. It can be illustrated by the following excerpt from the clinical practice of the first writer. A patient related the following story (details have been modified to prevent possible identification with any actual person, living or dead):

> "I have been considered a nice looking man. In a new community before buying a car I rode taxis frequently, to shop and so forth. There was a very attractive girl taxi driver who frequently picked me up.
>
> "On one occasion she said, 'I get asked out a lot by men passengers, and if I like the guy I will go.'
>
> "I see you wear a wedding ring. How does this fit with your marriage?"

"'Oh, I love my husband and he loves me. But he is a handsome guy—like you—and I know that whenever he is thrown with girls that want him and give him the eye he's right there on them. He'd poke it in any crack that showed itself. So why should I sit home with the TV—especially when everything on it is about men poking it where it don't belong? No, for every two or three girls he hops in bed with, I'm going to have at least one man myself. In other words, I do take it lying down.' Then she smiled that smile at me."

"And did you take advantage of it?" (the therapist asked).

"That's not necessary to know for therapy, Doc."

"It's none of my business, of course, but the more of this sort of your business you make mine, the more I can help you."

"I don't need any help at this time."

"Then why are you here? The truth is that you do need help, because you have a conflict between what you do and what you think you should do. But the fact that you are trying to convince yourself that you don't need help means that you are sealing the feelings of need for help off from the feelings that you don't need help. You try to carry these inconsistent feelings in separate 'logic-tight compartments' of your mind, and you don't think of them both at the same time."

"Doesn't everyone have some conflicts like that?"

"Yes, and they, like you, usually keep these conflicting thoughts in separate compartments."

This incident points out how the girl's husband had reached the SEXUAL SATIATION EFFECT. The girl was also becoming satiated, though she did not have logic-tight compartments. She was aware of the marital inconsistency. It didn't bother her or her husband, but it did bother the patient who reported it. The point for both man and wife, however, is that unduly repeated sexual intercourse without any feeling of commitment—in other words, "raw" sex for itself with loss of any real sense of relationship—results in failure of sex to be satisfying. Overly repeated sex relations between any partner can reach a "burn-out" state, which causes people of either sex to think in terms of variation of partners. It is not an easy psychological problem to handle in many cases. Some couples seem never to experience it, while others feel it chronically. In order to maintain the marriage vows it is often necessary to examine this **satiation effect** and find ways around it. This can be done if both partners really want a monogamous relationship.

The way they can do it is by thinking back over the early manifestations of their relationship and noting the factors that created an attraction at that time. Quite commonly couples doing this will see that both have let themselves slide in maintaining sexual attractiveness. Here a sort of re-birth can usually be accomplished by attention to the details of the early attraction.

And this is not just for the young. Couples of all ages experience the same problem and can find the same kind of solution. In fact, the longer a relationship has persisted the more difficulty it may be in. Witness the number of marriages that break up after twenty or thirty years or longer. Often it is important to think up some new sources of attraction and bring them into the picture. Over the years interests may have changed and new avenues of attraction may need to be created. Couples who really desire to maintain their relationship can work around this satiation effect by creative thinking in the whole area of romance.

All seriously committed couples should become aware of the **satiation effect** as sooner or later it is likely to become a problem. Anticipating it in advance will go a long way in making the solution easier.

As you enter the process of exploration of your over-all life experiences with the challenge of perceiving new possibilities, new angles, new opportunities to grasp advantages which you have not seen before, you will inevitably be snagged by some events which have been very negative and may seem at first to defeat you now. So we've got to neutralise these before going further.

In facing grief, sorrow, depression, or situationally caused emotional trauma—such as divorce, or loss of a loved one, career, health and so forth, major aids for most people are periods of meditation or prayer, quiet removal from external stimulation, followed by gathering of family, friends, and social activities which now counteract the internal withdrawal and create entrance to practical present life.

For the religious person, here is a place for religious faith to shine in aiding adjustment, provided the griever is truly religious and not merely a member of some religious group as a sort of "fire insurance" policy or as a means of gaining some kind of public or group acceptance or social approval. For truly religious people there is, however, herein a certain *caveat*. Here we must first note that most people are religious in at least the broad non-theological sense of *spirituality*—an emotional reaching for meanings in the inspirational and aspirational aspects of life, including the things we most cherish, the relationships of most value to us, the causes that most challenge us. Even those who abhor religious terms and common religious concepts and emphasis on their personal state of disbelief usually come under this generic heading of *spiritual* beings. For those in this class the **caveat** (or warning) may not threaten enough to create concern but there is at this point something of which to be aware:

Some religious people facing a great and especially an unexpected loss may have developed a dependency on a higher power. Most of them would probably call it God, and they would be prone to depend on it to bail them out of every trouble. Then when it does not give them everything they ask for or even what they desperately need they become devastated, angry and rebellious; they lose faith completely and join the atheists or at least the agnostics.

Many times the most faithful rebel in this way and cry out

to God, "Lord, I've tried to serve you, but now you are taking me to the wrong place, the opposite of where I prayed to go. So if you won't help me achieve my goals in life what good are you to me? You've dumped me when I needed you most, but I'll get even with *you*. I'll just stop believing in you and turn to a strictly secular way of life, maybe even an antireligious life."

Of course religious persons who do this merely compound their tragic losses: Now they must deal not only with the loss for which they asked help, but also with the shattering disappointment at not receiving this help. If you will think back over your own life, you will most likely recognize this pattern in more than one person whom you have known. And when you reflect upon these lives, you will probably see that they claim to have become enlightened, to have risen from the mire of superstition to the mountain of self-assurance that every strong person should have. They may even brag with the song that goes, " . . . . I need no God." But of course if they were actually religious, they are only kidding themselves.

So how do the turn-abouts fare in the long run? Sometimes they fare quite well for a number of years—or until another real tragedy overtakes them. At that point they usually split into two groups: Those who really can hack it without any spiritual support, and those who can't. The vast majority fall into the latter group. Many in this category break down completely and have to be admitted to an institution for care; others become self-assured in appearance and action, while expressing anger and frustration toward every aspect of the environment, although in a *sub-rosa* or covert fashion.

The few who really can make it without any help from a higher power or any one else live out their lives with varying degrees of success, although many of these show marked personality deficits. Of course many in the Power's camp also wind up psychopathologically, but the percentage is much smaller. If religion is used as an escape from facing reality it inevitably fails; if it is used as an assisting step in dealing with reality it usually succeeds. Without the havens of social and individual help which deal with and express the *spiritual* side of life most people end up in emotional states of poor adjustment which destroy happiness, health and occupational and social success. This is by no means to suggest that only those who follow the "old time religion" make it efficiently through life. Keep in mind the difference which we have noted between *religious* and *spiritual*.

So what are the final answers for (a) the nonreligious person, and (b) the person of faith? The *nonspiritual* among the nonreligious have to pull security, self-confidence and self-esteem out of a magician's hat unless they come by these traits through fortunate combinations of heredity and environment; otherwise they fall in a hole. The *nonecclesiastical* among the nonreligious (those who react negatively only against theological systems and not against the concept of a higher power *per se*) may make perfectly good adjustments. And of course people of faith may do the same *if* they observe the referenced *caveat*.

Now it is time to give this caveat a name: *The Caveat of Misplaced Expectation*: We must beware of expecting a higher power to do everything for us, especially everything in our prayers and supplications. Why are religious people faced with tragedy? (The question is basically that of Rabbi Kushner's *When Bad Things Happen to Good People*. Why? He answers, because, [for example] a germ doesn't know the difference between a good and a bad person. A hurricane or tornado does not know the difference. An earthquake does not know. And so on). But let us go a step farther and note why a higher power may have set things up this way:

It is apparent that if the power is "real", and if that upon our prayerful command he (or she or it) really gave us whatever we wanted, or even everything which we may at times desperately need, we would then be in control of it rather than its being a father to us. We would have become equal to it as a co-existing power. And what happens when two strong beings become of equal rank in a very responsible position? Almost always they get into a competitive clash. The ancient Hebrews realized this; therefore the *Shema (Hear, Oh Israel, the Lord thy God, the Lord is one)*. There was to be no scene wherein Yahweh stood on Mount Horeb and Thor on Mount Olympus shooting lightning bolts at each other. No, we couldn't become a successful co-god. Some power has to be the *Higher Power*.

At the turn of he twentieth century the Scottish Divine, Henry Drummond, wrote a book entitled *Natural Law in the Spiritual World,* in which he expressed a thesis a hundred years ahead of his time: God is part of nature and the natural world, and as such must obey his own laws. It really is a physically monistic world as the scientists insist. Francis Bacon predicted of this natural world: *Nature enim non imperitur nisi parendo*. (Nature's laws cannot be broken; they must be obeyed.) We can violate these laws, but they then break us. Thus if we leap off a skyscraper even a higher power cannot reverse the laws of gravity for us. But this power *can* bring into play *other* natural laws of which we may not be aware: A sudden gust of forceful wind around a tall building may drop us gently onto the huge awning of a first floor hotel. No natural law has been broken, but the *subjective* perception is that a supernatural event has occurred.

If we remember these facts, we can handle the situation when we grieve for help that is not granted. In the long run this ability to face and master a tough situation gives us strength to handle others. If we were always granted the *easy* way out we would eventually find ourselves *in control but too weak to go on*, even in the face of simple daily obstacles. We would become mindless beings whose place in nature could not be justified even as an endangered species. We would join the do-do bird in extinction.

So—while we should not welcome suffering, and certainly not attempt to bring it on ourselves—we can see a meaning and purpose in it and thereby turn it to our advantage. Along the way we can find help in some of the points and principles which others in like situations have found useful:

Patricia L. Fry, a free-lance writer of Oji, California, suggests (in *Columbia Magazine*, November 1989) principles which can help you receive or give comfort:

1. DO:

   a. Spend time with the individual. Just be there; don't worry about words. Cry if you feel like it. Express your own feelings, and let the sorrowing person cry or express other feelings.
   b. Express sorrow at the loss.
   c. Let the bereaved make decisions without feeling the pressure of your own thinking.
   d. Be a good listener. The process of *catharsis* is fundamental in all forms of psychotherapy.
   e. Help the sorrowing person to stay in touch with reality: to accept, by progressing at his/her own pace, the realistic situation and to go on in spite of it.
   f. Recognize the need for periods of silence: accept periods of withdrawal for a time.
   g. Assist where assistance is really needed, such as help with meals, and so forth.
   h. Spend time with the individual. Just be there; don't worry about what to say.

2. DON'T:

   a. Try to answer unanswerable questions, such as "Why did this have to happen to me?" We have already noted the philosophical and theological thoughts that may arise, and an approach to them that may help. But don't lay them on this person at this time. No provable answer is felt, so don't try to establish

one. You can explore all sorts of possibilities if the individual shows an interest in doing so, but don't push this beyond his/her motivation.
b. Say you know just how somebody feels—even with the same basic problem everyone's feelings will be a little different.
c. Try to keep one from expressing feeling in his/her own way.

Christopher News Service No. 289 quotes Dr. Phyllis Silverman of Harvard Medical School as follows:

1. Some authorities indicate that there are as many as ten steps in grief. But others like Dr. Rita Broadly, a widow who founded a support group, reduce the process to three: Initial shock, period of suffering, and recovery.
2. The grieving person may experience anger, guilt, depression, denial, withdrawal, loneliness, disorientation, restlessness, lack of energy, anxiety, panic, hostility, and combinations of many of these emotional states.
3. People experience trauma in many different ways. Men find grief more difficult than women, perhaps because men have been taught to suppress emotions.
4. Claire Booth Luce is quoted as noting that grief has a great purgative value.... It is like a bonfire which consumes all of the trash of life.

There is in the literature on grief a point of view which notes: There are four stages of grief:

1. Shock and denial (I can't believe it)
2. Anger (Why did this so unjustly happen to me?)
3. Guilt (What did I do to let this happen?)
4. Depression

The steps don't occur in a linear (straight line) fashion. We go through them in a rather haphazard way, and no two people experience them in exactly the same sequence of details.

We grieve most severely in cases of untimely death, divorce, loss of job, or loss of health.

We can adjust to our losses by:

1. Accepting their reality.
2. Experiencing and expressing emotions.
3. Reorganizing our lives without the element of loss.
4. Finding or organizing a support group of people with similar losses.

This chapter has no formal exercise because it deals with feelings which should not be put into a frame of practice until occasions arousing them occur—hopefully seldom. But when they do occur, review of the methods of dealing with them which are presented herein will help you to select procedures which will offer relief and hasten recovery.

So now proceed to Chapter V, Step 3.

Chapter V

Step 3

Developing Self-Confidence

*The text for this chapter is taken by permission from
Chapter 5 pp. 74-82 of* **Everything to Gain** *by
James C. Crumbaugh, Ph.D.
Chicago: Nelson-Hall, 1973.*

TO DEVELOP SELF-CONFIDENCE one excellent way is to develop the habit of *acting as if*—acting as if we were the successful, self-confident, capable person we would like to become. It goes a step beyond Norman Vincent Peale's "power of positive thinking" to **the power of positive action**. We first think positively by imagining what kind of person we would like to be. Then we act positively by doing at least one thing such a person would do. The more we act this way, the more we feel the part; and the more we feel it, the easier it is to act it. Soon it becomes ingrained in us, and we are no longer acting. The general idea of this procedure was suggested to me by an old book, *The Philosophy of As If*, by H. Vaihinger (New York: Harcourt-Brace, 1924). I developed the idea as an exercise and had been using it with patients for several years before I discovered a similar concept in *Wake Up and Live* by Dorothea Brande (New York: Simon and Schuster, 1936). The value of this approach has also been pointed out by Maxwell Maltz in *Psychocybernetics* (Englewood Cliffs, N. J.: Prentice-Hall, 1960). To make this procedure clear, let us take the case of Dan Ross who successfully practiced it.

"This summer you are working with the city park service, right?"

"That's right. I am part of a crew that goes around to the various parks and sets up playground equipment and builds baseball diamonds and tennis courts."

"Do you have much contact with the public?"

"You mean the sidewalk superintendents? Sure, they stand around giving us a lot of free advice about what to do and where. They all think they know more than we do. They bug me."

"Good. That's just the kind of situation for you to start with, because you will be able to see progress almost from the beginning. Now I'll tell you what I want you to do. Start out simply at first, just five minutes a day. It's somewhat like Alcoholics Anonymous. They don't expect members to pledge to quit drinking suddenly and permanently. They ask them to pledge to stop for only a day and to renew their pledge each day. Gradually the alcoholic extends the length of time of his pledge, but he takes the pledge for only as long as he is sure he can make it. In your case, Dan, you cannot expect to start suddenly 'acting as if' you were the personality you want to become and to maintain this action constantly. So begin with only a short interval. Anybody can make it for five minutes. And you can even pick out which five minutes during the day you want.

"So, for five minutes each day, while you're on the job, use your imagination and picture yourself as the successful, self-confident, secure person you want to become. Try to imagine how you would feel, think, and act. If you were all that you want to be, how would you behave? During this five minutes, you *are* your future self—the self you want to be. *Feel* yourself into the part, just like the method actors do. During this brief interval, you are to respond to whatever goes on around you just as you would respond if you had achieved the personality you want. Do you understand?"

"I don't know," the boy reflected. "You mean—like I am on the job and the foreman bugs me, I am supposed to keep my cool?"

"That could be one example, if the personality you would like to become would remain cool at all times. Would he?"

"I guess so. That's the way a person's supposed to be, isn't it?"

"That's not the point. The important thing is what you want to be. Do you need to be cool in order to get where you want to go in life?"

"Well, yes, at least most of the time."

"Actually you've done well on the job; so you must have handled the problems there pretty well."

"Anybody could do that on this job."

"You're running yourself down again and forgetting your assets. But all of us could use a little more cool, so let's assume that this is a goal for you. The important thing, however, is not to try to list all of the specific traits you would have, but just to *feel*—in your imagination—that you are the person you'd like to be. Then react to whatever happens as you feel such a person would. In this way the traits that you really will need will automatically and unconsciously come to be practiced, and you'll grow into you ideal self without ever having to study all of these traits."

"I don't know. I don't think this would work for me. I'm no good at acting."

"You don't have to worry about that. Everybody's a ham at heart, but you don't have to be an actor. You just act natural—except that you act as the self you want to be in the future."

"How can I do this on the job and keep my work going right?"

"Once you get the hang of it, your work will be made easier. But don't expect to do this all at once. Start with just five minutes. Suppose people stand around and give useless advice. Try this procedure with some of them. When you're bugged by their presence, take this five minutes for fantasy. If you had achieved the position you want in life, you would feel magnanimous toward everybody, and little things would not bother you nearly as much as they do now."

"I just can't see myself feeling big-hearted toward those sidewalk superintendents. I'd like to kick them."

"But before you think about that, try five minutes of feeling that you're the secure person you want to be, the person who can handle easily anything that happens. Practice this for just five minutes each day when they bother you, and in the next session tell me what happened. Will you do this?"

"I'll try. But I don't think it will work."

"Just try."

And this is what we would say to you, the reader, at this point. Just try. And while you are doing it, turn to the **Power of Freedom Exercise** for Step 3, and follow the directions there. Do some of this exercise along with the **act as if** procedure. You will find they work easily and effectively together in building self-confidence.

At the next session with Dan, after the usual pleasantries were exchanged, I said firmly, "Well?"

"You mean about the assignment you gave me?"

"Yes."

The young man tried to evade my eyes; then all at once he broke into a wide grin. "It works after all, Doc; I have to admit it really works. I tried this *act as if* when some people came up to watch. I bit my tongue and smiled at them, and I said something about how it was going to be a nice park. Then one guy started to complain about the way everything was run down because the city politicians were filling their own pockets instead of spending tax money for the public. I started to tell him to split. But then I thought I'd get my lesson done first. So I kept smiling and asked him about what he thought we could do about the situation. He raved on for a while, and then he cooled down. I could see that it did him a lot of good to say all those things, and then I saw that he didn't look mad at me like most of them usually did. So I felt better, and when he left, I could tell that he liked me, and I sort of liked him."

"Fine. You did well. If you'll just keep practicing this exercise, you'll be surprised at how much it will change your life."

"Yeah. I like it; so I got to doing it off and on during the day. It helped to pass the time, and I kept it up. It's pretty cool."

Dan did continue to do especially well with this procedure, and he rapidly improved. Soon his feelings of self-doubt, depression, and the inadequacy were very noticeably reduced. He was able to go on to the step of finding his "thing," an organized plan for his life that would fulfill his human need to be Somebody.

Another illustration of the effectiveness of this *acting as if* technique is found in a story about a bus driver. He violated what appears to be a national bus drivers' code: He was polite to the riders. One day a patron asked him why.

"Well," he explained, "another driver I knew was nice to a little old lady who reminded him of his mother. She seemed so helpless. Usually she had barely enough money in her purse to pay the fare. But when she died, it turned out that she was a wealthy woman with no heirs; and she left all of her money to him. So I thought that maybe if I tried that, I'd be lucky, too.

"It hasn't happened so far. But I noticed something funny. At first it was hard to be nice to people. I had to fake a pleasantness I couldn't feel. But when I acted nice, I found that a lot of people were nice to me too. This made me feel better in spite of the drudgery of jockeying this bus around in the madhouse traffic, and pretty soon I really did feel more pleasant toward most riders. I wasn't acting any more. And the better I felt, the better the riders seemed to feel toward me, and in turn the better I felt about them.

"It sure makes driving a lot easier, and I guess the customers must think it makes riding a lot easier too. Some of them take this bus instead of another one that takes them home by a shorter route."

This, then is the exercise of *acting as if* in action. To make it work, **your act** always has to come first. but once you start the wheel in motion, you'll find it is a **flywheel**, which develops its own momentum. And that is what carries you forward.

A word of caution here: This is not to condone acting as if you were something you should not or could not be. Untalented persons cannot become artists by acting as if they were one. This is where many of the pseudosophisticated go wrong. You cannot gain respect by acting as if you had done something worthy of it when you have not. This would simply be narcissism, which would defeat the very goal you wish to gain. The correct approach is to act as if you were the personality you want to be and should be—not as if you had already gained the achievements that you might wish or may in the future attain. Act as if you were Somebody, not because of great achievements, but because you are you.

Act as if and you will be surprised to find that you will soon come to believe it true. And it then will become true. The only reason the opposite has been true up to now is that you have believed and acted as if it were so. It is just as easy to move over to the other side, the desirable side. Try it and you will become convinced. But you must be prepared for an initial period of discouragement during which you won't yet believe in yourself and will have to depend strictly on the process of acting as if you believe.

You cannot change your feelings at will. What you can control through will power is behavior. Thus, the place to start is with the power of **positive action**. Act as if you were what you wish to become. You can make yourself do this even though you may not believe in it at first. Accept it initially on faith, and after a short time you will see the results. Then you will automatically begin to think positively. And the Bible tells us,

"As a man thinketh in his heart, so is he." You will then become what you wish to be. The results all depend on your getting started, and here is where you need the philosophy of "as if." You will be amazed at the results.

Dramatic success in the use of this technique was recently reported by a patient who is a minister: "I've been getting along fine now, especially since I realized that the philosophy of 'acting as if' has wide application and decided to apply it everywhere I could. Since then I have not needed a doctor of any kind. Before I tried your method I had some thought of suicide. Then I thought, it's just as easy to act as if I would *not* commit suicide as to act as if I would. So I have acted this way and have since felt fine.

"Also, I've done what I knew all along I should do—I worked to get people into the church. I've known what I should do, but I've never before had a commitment to do it. Part of my trouble has been that I have been floundering around without a clear purpose or goal. But now I'm feeling a challenge, and it can be a lifetime proposition."

This minister had long held a basic value system, but he only now had experienced the true encounter that could drive him to commitment to these values.

Similar success was reported by another male patient: "I was pleasantly surprised to find that the philosophy of 'acting as if' really works. At first I thought it was only a variation of the 'power of positive thinking' (in spite of what you said to the contrary), but I concluded I'd try it anyway. So I walked down the street with my chin out and shoulders back, as if I were just the guy I'd like to be. And right off I caught a couple of admiring glances from two cute girls, something I've never noticed before. Yes, I'm sold on 'acting as if'; it stops your daydreaming and makes you step out."

From there on this patient did step out. He is now finding a set of values and a commitment to them; he is beginning to feel and act like Somebody. And neither patient nor therapist could ask for more.

A college professor in therapy reported as follows on this method: "The 'acting as if' idea really works—you've got something there. I think it is especially good for somebody in teaching, where if you *act as if* you felt confident the students respond favorably. I have felt exhilarated since doing it."

In order to help you apply it, let us analyze what happened in the case of Dan. Let's see what went on within his personality as he learned to do this.

You remember that as Dan first evaluated his life he felt worthless. Then I explored his successes, and gradually he saw that he had been more successful than he had realized. Now it was time to establish new habits of accomplishment that would enable him to find a new sense of purpose in life. This was done by his *acting as if* he were the success he wanted to be.

In order to do this he had to break the vicious cycle which he had established—and which most people who lack self-confidence establish: (a) He failed in something; (b) he felt worthless as a result; (c) he therefore failed in still further areas because his feelings of self-deprecation consumed his energies and made consistent application of effort difficult; and (d) this failure cycle spiraled upward in intensity until he felt hopeless and helpless. His negative attitudes would be conveyed to others, who in turn would react to him as if he were the complete failure he felt himself to be. And all of this occurred in spite of the fact that his life was actually filled with many successes, which he was overlooking in his despair.

To break this vicious cycle the process had to be reversed, and there was only one way to do it. Dan himself had to initiate the break by believing in the **act as if** technique enough to believe that he could apply it to success if he really tried. Fortunately his earlier experience with it furnished this belief. He was able to start a reverse cycle of success by *acting as if* he were the success he wanted to become.

This procedure is reflected in an old adage, "Nothing succeeds like success." In other words, just as failure breeds failure, success breeds success. The trick is to get a start in the direction of success, and this is where Dan's trust in the **act as if** procedure gave him the necessary motivation to try hard enough to get this start.

Now you are ready to apply this procedure. If you will try it honestly, just as Dan did—even though you may at first be skeptical, just as he was—it will work for you as it did for him, and for the others whose cases have been quoted. Start out simply, just a few minutes a day, and during this brief interval imagine that you really are the successful person you want to become. During that time do everything just as you think such a person would. Maybe all you do at first is to walk down the street. How would such a person walk? If you pass someone, how would this person pass? Do just what he or she would do.

Repeat this procedure daily, even if it is for just several minutes. You will find, as Dan did, that once you start, it will become easy and interesting, and the problem of lengthening the period of practice will take care of itself.

Do not expect it to work miracles all at once, although you are likely to notice a positive effect almost from the first.

I know that if you stick with it, it will work. I know, not only because of ten years' experience in using it with patients and others whom I have counseled, but also from my own personal experience with the exercise. In fact, I developed it from personal experience. There have been two periods, each lasting over a year, during which I needed, in order to carry on professionally, to develop traits of personality that were adequate to meet the situations involved. I found that it was only when the chips were down and I was under pressure to do or die that I would really make myself do this; but I also found that, when I tried, I could do it. It has carried me through difficult times, and it can do the same for you.

One of my patients reported fantastic success with the technique. "I thought this 'acting as if' business was just another mental exercise," he said. "I didn't take it seriously until I went to apply for a job yesterday. All at once I realized that although

I was shaking inside and insecure, I had to act as if I were the perfect guy for the job. I did, and I got the job."

And you can *act as if* just as effectively. Remember that this is a continuing procedure, and that your record of it should be extended from time to time as you experience progress. When you feel you have gained a foothold on its use, and when you have done the **Power of Freedom Exercise** which will add to your self-confidence you will be ready for Step 4, **Getting Into the Mindset Necessary for Discovery of New Meaning and Purpose.**

Chapter VI

Step 4

Getting Into the Mind-Set Necessary for Discovery of New Meaning and Purpose

IN ORDER TO progress in discovery of new and more dynamic meaning in life, and to grasp new purposive goals to satisfy our deepest meaning we need to develop new techniques of attack or procedures in ferreting out the goals to fulfill this meaning. There are two basic special techniques which, when practiced consistently, will enable us to do this. They are designed to bring out the creative abilities that we all have in much greater degree than we usually realize, but which we don't learn to use. These techniques are as follows:

1. Expanding conscious awareness, and
2. Stimulating creative imagination.

Let us consider each of these and how it works. First, *expanding conscious awareness*: This means that we must become more aware of the world about us and what goes on in it. For example, if we ask you to look out of the window and tell us what you see, you may reply, "It is a sunny day, and a car is passing by, and there are two children playing in the yard." But if we ask you to take a second look and tell us what else you see, and if we add to your motivation by offering you a reward for each additional thing you can report, you will undoubtedly notice much more than you did the first time.

That is the way it is with our problems. If someone asks us what is wrong, we give a short answer and think that we have said all there is to be said. We don't like to talk about it in the first place, so we say a few words and try to leave it at that. But only by digging into the minute details—by expanding our conscious awareness of the vital and significant implications of the problem—can we hope to work out a new solution to it.

The truth is that this is exactly what many young people are talking about and trying to do when they blow their minds with various harmful drugs. They want to expand their conscious awareness and to see more of life than they have ever been able to see before. And their aim is a good one; the error is in their methodology. Their techniques lead to disastrous side effects and after effects. And in the long run the drugs don't accomplish their goals: They only give a false feeling that you have had some great insights into some new aspect of life; but when the drug effects wear off, these insights are gone.

There is, however, a safe and effective way to expand conscious awareness which we will consider presently.

Second, *stimulating creative imagination*: This is the process of using the creative capacity we all have in potential form. After we have expanded our conscious awareness to become more perceptive of what goes on around us, we need to use these new perceptions creatively. This means that we must put all of our experiences together in new ways, in order to find new meanings in the total pattern of life. When we have analyzed our problems in greater detail and have become aware of all of the aspects we may have previously overlooked, we then must relate all that we have found to the totality of our life experience.

This will suggest something new about where we should go from there.

In other words, we use our creative capacities to imagine new solutions to old problems. We do this through relating the new aspects of these problems (of which we have now become aware) to other areas of life (of which we have now also become newly conscious). Such a process puts our problem in a new light and gives us new hope for the future.

And then, without realizing just how it happened, we find ourselves in possession of a new lease on life, a new meaning and purpose, in place of the old feelings of hopelessness and despair: We have achieved the goal of logoanalysis.

The exercises given in this book for both of our two basic techniques will guide you in applying logoanalysis to your particular problems. But first let's turn to an analogy that will illustrate how it all works.

Imagine that your entire life is represented by a large picture. Further suppose that this picture is cut up into a thousand small pieces like a jigsaw puzzle. You have been trying to put the picture together and have succeeded in properly placing most of the pieces, but there are a number of missing segments.

These pieces represent missing elements of your life. That is, they are the failures, conflicts, and troubles with which you are now faced.

In some cases you may be able, at a later date, to find at least a portion of the missing segments. But right now, you don't know where they are, and you see no hope of locating them. In other words, as you view your present troubles, they seem to leave gaps or holes in your life, and you are unable to conceive of any way of filling them.

What if you are never able to find the missing pieces? You may be tempted to draw the conclusion that your life is hopeless and meaningless and that you have nothing left to live for. When you are faced with a severe problem, you will be concentrating on it so completely that you will ignore all of the other aspects of life, even though you may have some very good things going for you.

Thus, you will forget about all of the hundreds of pieces of your life that do fit together and give a real meaning and purpose to the overall picture. You will find it difficult to see the overall picture, although you may be looking right at it, because you are wrapped up in the little segment that represents some current problem.

When the problem is severe, you don't think about anything else at the time. This is very similar to what you would experience in looking at the picture through a long cardboard tube. Suppose you are looking through such a tube at the part of the picture that is circled and that represents your most severe problem. The tube is like the emotional upset that keeps your attention focused on this area of trouble.

Since you can't see anything else except your current trouble, you get the feeling that this is all there is to your life. If this were really true, it would be logical for you to give up in despair, for there would be too many missing pieces to allow you to find much meaning in the few remaining segments in this area. As long as you are looking through the cardboard tube at this one area of your life, as it were, there doesn't seem to be much hope for you.

But suppose someone comes along and knocks the tube out of your hand. Suddenly you see the whole picture of your life at once. Obviously you now see new elements of experience that remind you of important things to live for in spite of your difficulties. You sense a new meaning and purpose in your life as a whole. By comparison, the missing pieces within the circle—which had loomed so large when you were focusing only on this area—now take on far less significance. You wonder how you could have become so wrapped up in this little area of your life that you ignored all of the successes, the hopes and ambitions, and the assets in the rest of it.

Unfortunately, in reality no one can knock this tube out of your hand so that you can see the whole of life at one glance.

At the moment, you are forced by circumstances to peer in despair only at the few pieces that can be seen through the tube. How, then, can you work out of this apparently hopeless situation? There is only one way.

That way is to move the tube slowly around, gradually scanning the total picture segment by segment, so that finally you can put all of the parts together and perceive the meaning of the whole. It is a slow process, and you may become discouraged if you do not always remember the final goal. Some of the segments you will look at will have little meaning within themselves, but it is only by relating each segment to every other one that the overall significance of the total picture can at last be perceived.

In other words, when you look at the little slice of life represented by your immediate problem, it seems overpowering and meaningless until you move by association to another area of your past experience, and to another, and to still another. In the long run you will see your successes, your strong points, and your assets—all of which give a new meaning to the whole, a new hope for the future, and minimize the present failures. When you begin to gain a new perspective on the total pattern of your life, you will begin to grasp a total meaning and purpose in life. Thus, you can use the present difficulty as a stepping stone toward a new tomorrow.

A failure can be turned into an asset in the long run when it is seen as a learning experience that helps you attain a future goal—a goal you may not have been prepared to achieve without the prior failure. In this sense, misfortunes can turn out to be blessings in disguise. But to make use of them you have to explore their relationship to all of the other experiences you have had, and only then will you see what they are supposed to teach you in relationship to your future goals.

This process of "moving the tube around" over the whole picture of life illustrates the two basic techniques of logoanalysis. That is, moving the tube is a matter of *expanding your conscious awareness* of all that has occurred in your past experience and of *stimulating your creative imagination* to put together these segments of past experience in a new and meaningful way. Using these techniques will suggest an ultimate direction or goal that can be achieved.

The exercises are designed to help you explore your life experiences in relation to your present situation. Using them will enable you to find the meaning of the total picture of your life. When you have found it, you will be able to go on from there, in spite of whatever handicaps and difficulties you may face, and to live your life in a way that will give you an identity as Somebody.

This does not mean that only those who have serious problems can profit from the procedures. Life may be going well for you, but you may still sense a need to improve, to find a fresh meaning, a higher purpose. If so, these exercises can help you do it. You may be looking down the cardboard tube, as it were, at a merely boring present situation. Exploring this situation in relation to the many other segments of your total life experience can give you a new perspective. You will see that, by following the exercises, you can achieve success.

So now turn to them. When you feel that you have done what they ask of you, we know that you will be ready to pursue the next chapter on **Encounter**, which we believe will offer you a real challenge in your over-all process of discovering a new and satisfying meaning in life.

Chapter VII

Step 5

Encounter

"Encounter": Relating to "Significant Others" of Both Sexes

"ENCOUNTER" OR RELATING to others who enter significantly into your life is the key to meaning in life. The strongest human paraphysiological (or psychological) drive is companionship or love or becoming a "person" (an individual with status in the world around one). This relationship need not be human; it can be with a pet or with a superhuman being (God privately, though it could be some sort of "angel"). The key is still with another being.

Kitty Armstrong was one of the most voluptuous females I have ever seen. Although she was not yet nineteen, she had had many sexual experiences. She had been intimate with most of the members of the high school football team, the police force, the fire department, and a number of her home town's influential older men.

Kitty was not really her name, of course, and neither was sex her professional game—she was strictly an amateur. And this estimate applied to all of her human relationships. She was alienated and lonely. Although she had had sexual intercourse with over a hundred men, she had never "encountered" a single one of them.

The existentialist uses the term encounter to indicate a deeply meaningful personal relationship. It is an intimate one-to-one exchange of feelings and mutual understanding. In contrast to a rational transmission of knowledge and information, it is an emotionally toned reaching by one person for response from and acceptance by another—a phenomenon of feeling rather than of reason.

While Kitty had probably had more practical knowledge of sex than Freud, Ellis, Kinsey, and Masters and Johnson, she knew nothing about people. She had been brought to the clinic by her mousy, passive-dependent mother, a straight-laced widow who said she had reached "the end of my rope; I just don't know what to do with the child." I was seeing the mother first in private.

"What do you mean?" I asked. "What has she done?"

"What has she done? She has been sleeping with the entire male population of our town! She's not a prostitute, Doctor. She's just a baby, and she doesn't realize what she's doing. She's such a good girl that she just can't hurt anyone by saying 'no.' She really wants to love everyone. That's what my husband—God rest his soul; he was deeply religious—taught her, to love everyone. But she doesn't understand about sex, and all of these vultures take advantage of her. Can't you do something to educate her on the divine meaning and importance of sex? I've tried, but she just laughs at me."

"I have the feeling that on the subject of sex she might give *us* an education," I replied. "You may have tried to impose upon her the meaning of sex that is valid for you, but she hasn't accepted that. Obviously it has a different meaning to her. Do you know this meaning?"

"The meaning of sex to her? It doesn't mean anything to her. That's the problem—it should mean something."

"I can assure you that it does. It means a great deal to her. You are probably right in thinking that it means nothing in and of itself. But symbolically and indirectly it means everything. It is the one channel through which she has found fulfillment of her other needs."

"Needs? What needs, Doctor? In spite of my being a widow and having to work hard, I've given her everything, even a car."

"Everything material, perhaps. But I am not speaking of material needs. It is obvious that your sacrifices have well supplied her materially. Have you stopped to consider, however, that man does not live by bread alone?"

"Of course I have!" The mother became angry. "I've harped on this very thing—the spiritual side of life—and that's what she has rejected."

"She has not rejected spiritual needs. But she does resent your trying to force her to accept your own spiritual meanings. She wants to find her own meanings—just as we all do, just as you did. No one else can find these for us."

"What's right and moral is true for everyone, and it's a parent's duty to teach the children."

"Kitty is no longer a child, Mrs. Armstrong. She's a young woman who thinks and feels for herself, not a robot to be programmed with the responses you wish her to make. This is one of the most common mistakes of doting parents, and it always produces resentment and alienation."

"Say, whose side are you on, Doctor? I'm the one who brought her to you, and the one who's paying you."

"I'm not on any side, but on all sides. You brought her to be helped. The only way she can be helped is through understanding, not through exhortation or command. Now, if she didn't get something she wants through sex, she wouldn't use it. It isn't money or material needs she wants, so she must be doing it to fulfill some psychological need. Of course, in rare cases there can be a medical reason that makes one overly responsive sexually; but Kitty, as you told me, has already had her medical and psychiatric evaluations, and they didn't turn up anything. So there is no question that the trouble lies in the psychological area. And here you cannot answer for her. Only she can tell us the trouble, and she won't do this in your presence. So I must talk to Kitty herself, and privately. And I'll tell you beforehand that everything she says will be kept strictly confidential. I'm not going to mention anything to you unless she gives me permission to discuss it with you."

Mrs. Armstrong unhappily muttered something about how poor widowed mothers were shown no respect or consideration, but she reluctantly went back to the reception room. From then on I interviewed the daughter.

The girl was, at first, no happier to talk to me than her mother had been to listen. I broke the ice with some innocuous questions about her school work and the like. Finally I began to probe.

"Kitty, just what does sex mean to you?"

"Sex? It's the most."

"The most what?"

"The most fun."

"Come off of it, Kitty. You know you don't really enjoy it with most men, do you?"

She was trapped, and she knew that I knew. But she defended herself. "The hell I don't. How do you know what I like? I'd rather have sex than eat. And I'll tell you this, I know more about sex than you and all of the square books you've got on those shelves. Ask any of the boys or men I've been with."

"So sex means power and prestige to you, doesn't it?"

She looked at me sharply, and then her defenses began to weaken a bit.

"I may not rate with the squares, but most men want what I've got to offer. I'll bet you'd like to have me right now."

"Certainly."

Kitty's eyebrows shot up, her black eyes glistened, and her lips curved into a wicked smile. "Okay, it's all right with me.

But don't give me any more about morals. You're no better than the rest."

"Men are all alike, aren't they?" I asked.

"They sure are," she said.

"Kitty," I said, "you asked me if I wanted you, and I said I did. I'm still alive. But I have no intention of doing anything about it. In the first place—if I had no other reason—we are well trained against this professionally. Obviously if I become emotionally involved with you, I can't help you. And even if I didn't care about this, the other professional risks would be too great. If I wanted an affair, a patient would be the last resort—even a patient of prime choice sexually, like you."

She was startled by what she thought was a sudden reversal of my attitude, but she didn't give up. She began to unzip her skirt. I arose and started for the door.

"If you don't stop this nonsense, I'll have to call your mother."

Kitty's eyes sparked. Now she thought she had me. "If you do, I'll scream and tear my blouse and say you attacked me!"

"That's up to you—if you think she or anyone else will believe you! You're not the first patient to try something like this. You've learned to use sex as the only means of controlling men—most of whom you obviously hate—and as the only means of getting the attention and acceptance you crave. Now you've tried it on me, but it won't work. Now will you sit down? Do we talk, or do I—?" My hand was on the doorknob, and I started to turn it. Then I hesitated, hoping she would stop me with a word of surrender.

Actually, this could have been a sticky situation. Sexual blackmail rarely occurs in the clinic; but when it does, psychotherapists must have a good prior reputation. My own observation is that—in spite of a popular impression to the contrary—violation of professional ethics by sexual involvement with a patient is rare among psychotherapists.

Kitty hadn't given up yet. She grabbed her blouse as if to rip it, and I opened the door. But when the chips were down, she lost her courage—for which I was thankful. The blackmail could have been handled, but it could have been a real problem, and I was glad that this wouldn't be necessary.

"All right, Doctor." She adjusted her clothes and sat down. "I don't know why, but I'm not going to do it."

I closed the door and returned to my chair. "You're not going to do it because deep down you know that I'm right about what I said, and that I want to help you."

She was silent. A tear started to form, but she resisted an emotional breakthrough and again took the offensive.

"You—you bastard! I'd like to spit in your face!"

"Of course you would, because you can't stand to face the facts that I've shown you. Deep down you know I'm right, don't you?"

She didn't answer. Then finally she mumbled, "Yes, damn it. Why do you have to rub it in?"

"Because only by your admitting to yourself just what you're doing to yourself can you change the picture."

"I like it the way it is."

"Do you? If you did, you wouldn't hate every man you sleep with. You hate them all because you know that in spite of the fact that they give you some favors in return, they are interested only in using you. And it all leaves you so nauseated with the male animal that you can't experience orgasm with any of them, not even when you meet a boy that you could really care for."

She looked at me painfully as I made the last statement, and I knew I had hit the truth. "You're really frigid, aren't you, Kitty?"

She stared straight ahead; then her defenses crumbled. She burst into tears.

"I'm glad you've finally let yourself cry, because you've needed this for a long time."

After a while she said, "Sure I'm frigid. The only time I can come is when I'm masturbating and thinking about a certain boy who's never even tried to make me. He's the only one who hasn't, and the only one I really want to do it."

"So what you want is a deep meaningful relationship, one

where you fully understand and care for each other. And you can't get that through sex. Once you have it, you can use sex to seal it; but you've got to start with the relationship, not with sex."

The girl nodded reflectively. After a while she said, "I wish my mother had done that with my dad. She was always so prissy, so goody-goody; she loved him, but she couldn't say it in bed, even married to him. She took care of him every other way; but she was so cold, I don't know how they ever managed to have a child." She choked on her words.

And then she was angry and shaking all over. "You want to know who started me on sex? You want to know? Well, I'll tell you. It was my old man—but it was all her fault. He'd get hot, but she wouldn't take care of him. He was so frustrated that he finally would get one of those magazines with the naked women in it, and he'd go in the bathroom and masturbate. I caught him once, when he thought the door was locked. I felt so sorry for him. I wanted to take care of him, but I'd never been with a man. Oh, a couple of boy friends and I had played with each other, but we didn't really do it. Sometimes when Dad came in to kiss me good night, I knew he wanted me bad, and I wanted him. He'd brush against my breasts, and then I'd brush them against him, and he'd get excited, I could tell.

"And then one night it happened. He thought I was asleep, and he fondled one breast, and I made out that I was sleeping sound. I let him think I was dead to the world, and finally he went all the way, but he held his body up off of me so he wouldn't wake me. I wanted to take him in my arms and kiss him and tell him to do it all night, but I didn't dare let on I knew what he was doing.

"But later when I thought about it, I realized that he took a chance on knocking me up, and I hated him for that. From then on I guess I had two different feelings for him. One part of me felt sorry for him and wanted to make love. But the other part wanted to take a butcher knife and castrate him. But tell me, Doctor, what's so bad about making your father happy if your bitchy mother won't do it? Anyhow, he died not long after that, and I said to myself that when I found a boy like my dad I'd marry him. But I've had hundreds, and like I said, they're all bastards except this one boy I told you about. Well, Doctor, are you shocked?"

"I may have been, the first time I heard a story like this," I answered, "but it has been so many years ago that I've forgotten. It's not everybody's life story, but it's not that rare. Most people think that whatever happens to them happens for the first time in history. Problems fall into types or categories. And while every case is in many ways unique, your general problem—the way you've been misusing sex to get what you really want in life—is quite common."

Gradually, over a period of about a month, I gained Kitty's full confidence. At last she was sure I wanted to help her. She now knew that I was not just a minion of her mother, and that I wasn't trying to change her life to conform with mama's dictates. I wanted only to help her find a style that would enable her to actualize the hidden needs for which she had unsuccessfully tried to substitute sex.

Finally, she faced the fact that the missing part of her life was the ability to be close to another human being, to accept, to trust, and to open her feelings to another person who would respond in the same way to her. In spite of her beauty—in some cases because of it—she had from childhood experienced only the insincere efforts of others to manipulate her feelings to their own advantage. Whenever she had trustingly let down her defenses, she had been crushed by the ultimate realization that these feelings had not been honestly accepted and returned.

She had often reached out for people, but she didn't know how. As an only child she had been indulged by her parents to the point of becoming something of a spoiled brat, and, of course, the inherent selfishness of this type of personality repelled others who might have offered a genuine relationship. The only contacts that remained to her were those of personalities similar to her own, which meant that each was trying to get more than was given. Soon she learned to trust no one, and she became an alienated and lonely girl.

And then, as she grew into womanhood, she had discovered the magical power of sex. By seduction she could obtain the superficial love of men, the envy of women, and the fulfillment of a thirst for power. This "love" was only as enduring as her sexual charm; and when this magic waned through familiarity, the pledges of undying devotion would quickly fade. But there was always a new lover to replace the one who left, and the cycle would be repeated. As her reputation spread, the length of the cycles narrowed; so that when she came into therapy few men dared to have sex with her more than once, for fear of their becoming identified with the town tramp. But for Kitty there was still the supreme power of that one night, with which she could rob most of the established women of their men.

Not that she really wanted the power. As logotherapy teaches, Adler's "will to power" is only a means to an end. When we don't find a purpose in life that offers us a personal identity as Somebody, we grasp for any kind of power that will enable us to manipulate our environment. We hope to hit upon some avenue of fulfilling the need that is frustrated.

Kitty's need for identity was the real source of her frustration. It was, therefore, the point upon which we had to focus in therapy. She had to learn to trust someone with her true feelings, and to offer in return a genuine acceptance of that person's emotional life.

"The only way I've ever been able to get anything I want," she wistfully admitted, "is through my body." Her eyes expressed a dread of the day when her body would no longer be appealing. Deep within she had for some time realized that she was playing a losing game.

The power of personal relationships to give meaning and direction to an otherwise confused life may be seen in the story of Alexander King, an illustrator and a former editor of *Life*. King, long addicted to narcotics as a result of medical prescription for intractable pain, married a beautiful girl. They adored each other. After several hospitalizations had failed to cure King's addiction, his wife offered—if he could not break the habit and must spend the rest of his life as a user of narcotics—to go with him to some foreign country where drugs could be obtained legally or without difficulty. This willingness to sacrifice so much for him so moved him that by sheer will power he quit using narcotics and never returned to them.

He, like all of us, had a potential power that he had not dreamed he could muster until a purpose for calling upon it became apparent. Then he rose above his former limits without knowing how. All he needed was a reason. A reason in this sense, however, is not just a logical reason—which he had always had, for logic told him that addiction was disastrous—but rather an emotional reason based on a deep sense of a worthwhile purpose in life. When he perceived that someone else could so love him as to suffer for him, he sensed a mission in preventing the necessity of that suffering. This kind of love showed him he was Somebody, and knowing that brings out the best in us all.

A logical place to begin is with friends and relatives. Of course, it is possible that you are in a strange surrounding with no people of your own. But if there are human beings in your environment, it is probable that at least some are potential friends.

The principle is always to make other persons need you; they will then be willing to fulfill your need for them.

Did you say you have no chance to meet people? There are opportunities awaiting you everywhere.

The stranger you need most to encounter may be a very familiar stranger—may, in fact, have been your husband or wife for years, and you may have never really met. If so, isn't it time to get existentially acquainted, to experience this encounter?

It may happen that the routine or past associations represented by family and friends are inadequate for the closeness you need because of the particular nature of your past experiences. It could be, for example, that the particular way of life that you have made your own through education, travel, or other experience is quite different from that of your early training. In this case you may have to look to new contacts. As an example, you may have become disillusioned with the beliefs of your family religion after learning some things in school that seem to conflict with these beliefs. So you quit going to church, and no longer feel close to the people there. But you have not found any new contacts to fill the void; you have been drifting instead, with a sort of empty space in this area of your life, never becoming consciously aware of this fact. If you learn more about both science and religion, you will find that there is no conflict. You may, however, decide that the old church no longer fulfills your religious needs and seek the old values in a new religious group.

This situation occurs frequently among college students. As a former college professor, the first writer had many occasions to counsel young people with this problem. The solution is to see that the values of a true religious experience are not bound to any one set of theological beliefs, and then to search for the form of religious expression best suited to your particular emotional needs. This inevitably involves building the relationship of a true encounter between yourself and religiously inclined people who hold the same values.

It may be that the main obstacle to a deep and genuine encounter with the people already in your life is a set of firmly ingrained habits that have become so automatic that you tell yourself you cannot break them. For example, perhaps you are so used to irritating people by a lack of tact that you justify yourself with the thought, "That's just the way I am and I can't help it." Then it is time to ask yourself a basic existential question: Have I really assumed responsibility for the course of my own life?

Have you genuinely believed in your own freedom to choose what you will make of it (within the limitations of heredity and environment)? Or have you let yourself off the hook by telling yourself that there is nothing you can do to solve your own problems and to straighten out your difficulties with people, and that all you can do is feel sorry for yourself?

If this is the case—and it usually is—the next step is to admit it and turn back to tackling the wall of resistance within. Turn once again to the relationships you want and need in your life, and take a long, second look. Search yourself honestly, expecting that you will unconsciously try to justify your efforts as doing all you could have done.

Ask yourself these questions: Have I blocked myself in my attempts to get close to the important people in my life? Have I fallen into the trap of long-established habits of escaping my own responsibility by telling myself I have been unjustly dealt with, unfairly treated, and that the failure isn't my fault? Think all of this through carefully. Is there some telltale evidence that you have not done all you could, that you have not assumed full responsibility for all of the choices that are open to you? For example, if you are tactless, have you tried your best to learn tact? Have you studied the way tactful people handle situations that give you trouble? Or have you deceived yourself into thinking that it is not necessary for you to change because it is the duty of others to accept you as you are? If you sense such marks of self-deception, start once again to struggle with the problem, and this time watch yourself every step of the way, repeating these questions to yourself at frequent intervals.

Now, if you have carefully examined yourself and concluded that you are not guilty of self-deception, that you have taken full responsibility for all you could do and that failure results from factors beyond your capacity to remedy, stop. Accept the fact that in nine of ten cases you are still rationalizing, still defending yourself, still being blinded by your own feelings of resentment of what life has done to you. Accept this and look once again at the encounters in which you have failed, at the problems that you have considered unsolvable. Again ask the question: Have I taken full responsibility for trying everything I possibly could, have I tested my ingenuity to the limit of its capacity?

If, after repeated trials, you have come to the point where you can say only that you have truly done your best within the area of all choices open to you, the next step is in order **after you do the exercises for this chapter.**

Chapter VIII

Step 6

"Dereflection": Defusing Liabilities and Infusing Assets

> The case quoted in this chapter is from the
> clinical files of the first writer.
> As always all identifying data have been changed
> to insure case privacy.

NANCY GOODMAN CAME for counseling because she was suffering from what Frankl calls the human condition of our times, **existential vacuum**. In spite of a full life for her thirty-five years, she was bored by the failure of a long struggle to find a meaning and purpose that would mark her as Somebody and give her existence a personal identity.

Nancy had read *The Doctor and the Soul*, the first of Frankl's books to appear in English, and she was deeply impressed by logotherapy. She was ripe for this approach to human existence, but she was green in applying it. Although she was not sick, she needed help. While she possessed the fullness of material success, she felt empty in spirit. And in spite of the ability to function well in the externals of daily routine, she was inwardly a hollow shell.

I noticed that she was very beautiful and poised the first time she came to see me. "How may I help you, Mrs. Goodman?" I asked as I glanced over the sheet of preliminary data completed by the receptionist.

"I'm hoping you can tell me, Doctor," she answered in a soothing, sultry voice. "I can't really say there is anything wrong. I have a rather full life with no special worries. I ought to be happy, but I'm not. I get so bored sometimes I wish I could take off for the moon. I feel like running from life, but there's no place to go."

I looked again at her data sheet. "You certainly seem to have attained a great deal of success as far as the usual values sought by most people are concerned."

"You mean that I've enough money for comfort, that I've had a successful business career, and that I've had the time to devote to my special interests. And, I suppose, that I've always been reasonably successful in whatever I've undertaken."

"Well, largely, yes. But you have failed in one area—marriage. You've had two unsuccessful marriages."

Nancy glared at me. "Oh, that. You seem to be assuming, Doctor, that we women live only for the glory of being accepted by men. Well, I've got news for you, Doctor. We females can make it just fine without men, and doing so is not a mark of failure."

"Agreed. But in that case, why did you want to marry in the first place?"

She resisted entrapment. "The first time I was young and didn't know any better, and I wanted to get out of the straight jacket in which my stuffy parents kept me. And the second time I found a man—the president of a large department store where I was the head buyer—who could have been a worthy husband. But he wasn't interested in sharing my life or in helping me develop my true potential. He was concerned mostly with his own achievements. He considered me only an expensive decoration, a luxury to take off the shelf and play with when the mood hit. I didn't feel at all bad about taking him in the divorce for enough to make myself comfortable. He had a good lesson coming."

"You sound rather vindictive. And this means you feel you are the one who failed, and that the other person came out ahead."

Nancy didn't like that remark at all. "No, I'm not vindictive. I really feel sorry for him. He doesn't know how to live; all he knows is work. In spite of his success, he has never found himself."

"But isn't this just what you said about yourself? In spite of your success, you haven't found what you want in life, have you?"

Nancy was silent, but it was the kind of silence that gives consent. I started again to review her case history.

The story of her past life was varied and exciting. She was the only child of middle-class Protestant parents. Her father was an accountant; her mother, a housewife. The family had been strictly establishment, a dutiful cog in the post-World War II "organization man" machine. For them the life goal was suburban security, with two cars under the carport and a boat on the lake; and the way to get these blessings was to line up with the *status quo* and its power structure.

For Nancy this was not only a life of boredom and meaninglessness, but also a hypocritical surface endorsement of traditional values that served only those in power. And she felt that such values were held in secret contempt and flagrantly violated by these same men and women. In high school Nancy began to disdain this hypocrisy; in college she broke into open rebellion; and in the business world she actively sabotaged the system.

As a college freshman and sorority pledge with bids from several sororities, she was popular with the fraternity boys. One of the males took advantage of her distress over a quarrel with the housemother and persuaded her to elope and marry. But within a few months she was disillusioned. He proved to be a rascal who wanted her to go to work and support him while he went to school. She went to the divorce court instead and then back to her family.

Returning to college, she majored in business administration, but upon graduation she found only secretarial work, for which she blamed sex prejudice. She had the initiative to find a way out, and within a year she became private secretary to the president of a large department store.

During the next several years she was a popular, but selective, woman courted by—among others—her aging multimillionaire boss. She diplomatically fended off his advances, while leaving him enough hope to keep open the door of any advantageous contacts he could offer.

Through one of these contacts she obtained a position as buyer with his chief competitor, the city's other big department store. Of course, her former boss was furious; in fact, he became so angry that he had a mild paralytic stroke and, as a result, had to relinquish the presidency to his son Kenneth. Unknown to the father and largely in defiance of him, Kenneth had also courted Nancy with the same dubious success.

A year passed, during which his son played a double gambit. Partly to retrieve Nancy from dangerous competition, and partly to prove his manhood to be greater than that of his father, he continued to pursue her. Nancy was no fool; she learned buying quickly and well. Without giving or promising herself, she accepted Kenneth's offer to return to the old company in the capacity of head buyer.

This outraged her former associates, subordinates with more experience and expectations of the position for themselves. It also caused her former boss, now retired, to have a second stroke. He died shortly thereafter.

Kenneth was now the chief executive and principal stockholder of the company, and this multiplied correspondingly his stock with Nancy. Within a year they were married, and she retired from an active company role.

Yes, she had learned to play well the organization man's game and to beat him at it. She was now the power behind the executive throne, and for a time she found a real personal identity in this role. She prodded her husband to greater and greater success, and when he faltered or stumbled, she put him back on course.

But she had made one fatal mistake: She had taught him too efficiently. For her, competitive success had been only a game at which she must prove herself superior. This was her answer to the galling early rejection of her feminine status. But for Kenneth these goals became ends in themselves, and he soon lost sight of his wife in the struggle.

At first she was so busy enjoying the power of her position that she did not notice what had happened. As the wife of one of the city's wealthiest and leading citizens, her advice, membership, opinion, and support were sought for many kinds of causes. Civic enterprises and social events, which previously would have been closed to her, now enlisted her in leading capacities.

And if she didn't find activities to her liking, she was in a position to create them. This she did not hesitate to do, even at considerable expense, for she had unlimited charge accounts and credit, and her husband was too absorbed in making money to notice how she was spending it.

So Nancy adopted and soon discarded a rapid succession of causes, ranging from a variety of charities, through free Sunday afternoon symphonies, Little Theatre, amateur opera, and psychic research.

As a young girl she had tried ballet dancing, acting, painting, writing, and singing. She had a little talent, but not enough to score well in any area. In response to a marginal awareness of this fact, she had been given to moods of depression and withdrawal. But her strong drive to be Somebody had always forced her out of a failed project and into something new.

The more she searched for fulfillment and failed, the more conscious she grew of the emptiness of her marriage, and the more nauseated she became by her husband who epitomized the values she held in contempt. She was resentful of his ignorance of, and unconcern for, her inner feelings of restless boredom—the boredom that signals the presence of Frankl's existential vacuum.

The outcome was hardly surprising. Before Kenneth realized what had happened, his wife and a sizeable chunk of his fortune had passed through the divorce court and out of his life.

Both he and Nancy were satisfied to go their own way. Kenneth was unhappy but did not know it because he was not aware that his life's passion for money and power was an inadequate substitute for a mission he had never found. Nancy was unhappy, but she knew it because she was aware that she needed such a mission, and had not found it. Of the two, Nancy was in the more hopeful position.

Following the divorce Nancy embarked upon a major effort to find herself. During the next two years she tried many things.

At first she thought politics would fill the void. She ran for the city council, and her charm captured votes. But she couldn't keep her mind on the town's business, and was gone on so many trips during meeting times that the council censured her. She seized the chance to resign and to blame antifemale prejudice.

Next, she decided to try religion. A natural reaction to her strict upbringing was to reject the confinement of the Judeo-Christian tradition and to turn to oriental thought. A logical direction was Zen Buddhism.

So Nancy read a lot of Zen and studied with an Indian Guru. But meditation upon a mystical *Koan* (such as, what is the sound of one hand clapping?) did not feed her need for literal soul food. Soon she dropped Zen.

She tried in rapid succession Christian Science (too ethereal), Spiritualism (too mystical), Baha'i (too square—no drinking, and all that), Reform Judaism (too selective—no dilettantes welcome), Catholicism (too establishment), and Unitarianism (too intellectual and emotionally antiseptic).

Maybe the spiritual union she sought could be found only

in a more concrete relationship. It occurred to her that this might materialize only in a truly fulfilling sex experience—perhaps a lover would bring her into harmony with the Eternal. She had had her fill of marriage, but she had never had a genuinely satisfying sex life. That's what was missing, she thought.

About this time, Nancy met Roger, an unconscionable scoundrel who persuaded her to accept him as her sexual partner. The affair lasted only a few months.

"What a slimy s.o.b. he turned out to be!" Nancy recalled. "I trusted him fully, and gave myself completely to him. When he put his arms around me, he was reaching for my checkbook behind my back. That's how he repaid me."

However, Nancy did gain some benefit from the experience. She discovered that sex was not the answer to her problem.

So what was the solution? Nancy was running down in her floundering quest. Finally, it occurred to her that she was running *from* something within herself, rather than *toward* something. Of course, she had marginally known this all along, but would not face it until she was exhausted from the flight.

This was when she came for help. After having read Frankl's book, which fortunately coincided with her exhaustion, she was ripe for the insight into what had been happening and for awareness that she needed guidance in working herself out of the fog.

"Let's see where we go from here," I said after we had discussed her case history. "You're looking for the right thing—a place to put your life that will pull the pieces together and give it a new meaning and purpose. But so far you've looked in all of the wrong places. What is left? Where else is there to look, that you have not yet explored?"

"I'm about out of ideas," she confessed, "but I have considered some other possibilities. For example, I might go back to school, and take all kinds of courses, until I find my thing."

"That's a partially good idea," I agreed. "It won't do the job alone, but you could undoubtedly profit—like most people—from a broader basic education. This is a fundamental source of ideas. You could attend adult education classes at night and on weekends, if you want to, so that you would have plenty of time for any special area of interest that develops."

"Yes, there are so many problems in the world today that anyone can find something that is special to him. But my problem seems to be that nothing lasts. I've been seriously interested in everything I've tried, and at first all of them seemed to be it. Then after awhile they would all fade, and I'd begin to be bored again, and disillusioned and restless, and I'd have to start over."

"Why do you think this happens? Why can't you maintain an interest?"

"I wish I knew, Doctor. That's why I'm here. Why doesn't anything last? What's the matter with me? Or is the world crazy?"

"The world's crazy, but that's not why you can't find yourself. Your basic problem is that you've tried to solve it by taking vacations."

"What?"

"I mean that you've tried to solve conflicts by running from them, just as if you took a vacation and expected the trouble to go away by the time you returned. Each of your safaris into the unknown in search of a purpose has really been an escape from facing what is missing in your life, rather than—as it seemed on the surface—a direct attack upon the problem."

"You mean that my real life purpose involved some obstacle I don't want to face? Yes, I've thought that at times, but I don't know what it is."

"It *is* an obstacle of which you're not aware."

"Well, what is it, for God's sake?"

"I don't know."

"You don't know! That's a big help. Thanks for nothing!"

"Simmer down, Nancy. I don't know—yet. And you don't know. But together we will find out."

"All right, Doctor. I don't know where you're going, but I'll go along for awhile."

"Good. Now I want to tell you the story of someone else who faced pretty much the same search for meaning in life with which you are struggling, and who experienced about the same frustration. As a matter of fact, a lot of people could give you a parallel picture."

"Really? I sort of thought—"

"You thought, as most of us do, that nobody else has problems just like yours."

"Yes, I guess—"

"Your experience is basically what Frankl calls the '**collective neurosis** of our times'—the existential vacuum left by a lack of a sense of meaning and purpose in life, due largely to the human condition today. It's something we all have to face and overcome in this computerized machine age. And we each run into our own special hang-ups in conquering it. There is no standard formula to deal with it; we have to tailor the answer to our own individual life experiences. And yours—like those of many other people—involve some special hang-up that has to be worked out before you can find your purpose. It is this hang-up that we have to uncover together."

"That sounds okay. But how?"

"I think you'll understand the problem better after I tell you this story, which will illustrate how human this struggle is, and how similar your feelings are to those of others who have faced it."

"Is this your own life story, Doctor?"

"No. Mine you'd never believe anyway. Do you know anything about Mount Kilimanjaro?"

"I think—it's a mountain in Africa, isn't it? Didn't Hemingway write something about it?"

"Yes. It is the tallest peak on the African continent. Rising about twenty thousand feet above sea level, it is perennially snowcapped. Animals seldom venture above the timber line, for there's no food or shelter and nothing they'd want. But in the twenties a party of explorers who succeeded in scaling the western summit found near the top the dried and frozen carcass of a leopard. No one has ever explained what the leopard sought at this altitude. But from this simple story, which appeared in the public press, Ernest Hemingway spun one of his greatest stories."

"Oh—yes, I think I remember a movie, something about the snow on that mountain."

"That's right. It was from Hemingway's short story, *The Snows of Kilimanjaro*. The story is only about nine thousand words long, but it contains in a nutshell the whole picture of man's search for meaning in life."

"I remember that the snowcapped peak was supposed to be some kind of a symbol of life to the hero."

"The hero was a writer, Harry, who had been unable to write for awhile. He seemed to have lost his creativity. In an effort to find inspiration, he returned on a safari with his latest mistress to an accessible level on Mount Kilimanjaro, because he had once been there during his most productive period. The mountain had become a mystical symbol of the elusive quality of meaning in life, the meaning Harry had struggled without success to find. He thought that once he was back on the mountain, things would begin to fall into place. But he contracted blood poisoning, transportation broke down, and his lover attempted to care for him while they sent for help. The help did not arrive in time, however, and he died. His last thoughts were a fantasy that a plane came to take him to the hospital. But after the aircraft took off with him, it suddenly changed course and headed directly into the snowcapped summit. As it was about to hit, Harry experienced a revelation that the peak contained the ultimate meaning of life, which he was at last going to understand."

Nancy was uncomfortable. "You are saying that I, like Harry, have been trying to find my way to the mountain top. Are you also saying that, like him, I'll find what I'm seeking only in death?"

"Not necessarily, although that's true of a lot of Harrys—there are many of him. In fact, Hemingway himself was probably the model for his character, for he struggled all of his life to attain this same knowledge of the ultimate values in human existence. He found what he considered at least partial answers that fit his own experience and gave it meaning, but the meaning was illusory and capricious—he could not maintain it consistently. At times he felt that all of his work worthless, and that nothing was lasting. In a fit of such despair he committed suicide."

"You think I might do that?"

"You have not shown this trend of personality so far. But you no doubt feel like checking out at times, just as most of us do. It all depends upon how you handle things from now on. You came for help because you are close to the end of your rope in the search for your own meaning. As we've said, your trouble lies in the fact that some hang-up, at present unknown, has kept you from finding a stable and permanent meaning for your own life. Now we must explore together in a systematic way all of the areas of human value in an effort to find, first, what you want that would give life meaning, and second what hang-up blocks this attainment. When we find where the problem is, we can work it out. Then you can settle upon a life goal that should be satisfying on a permanent basis."

"What do you mean—explore in a systematic way all human values?"

"That's what we are coming to. I am going to give you a series of exercises as homework assignments."

"You mean it's going to be like going back to school?"

"These exercises are quite grown-up. There is no mental strain—although you may sweat emotionally at times, because they will lead you to face yourself and your real, deepest inner feelings, and this often isn't pleasant. This type of homework isn't the school kind—although, as you yourself suggested school might not be a bad idea for you. While we are working, why don't you take a couple of courses in the university extension department? It might be best not to take the courses for credit.

Since you already have a degree, the university will let you audit courses. Take courses in such things as literature, science, history, sociology, and the like, because they will help you get a broad picture of the whole panorama of human experience, and that is what you need."

"Yes, but don't you think I should also take some psychology and philosophy?"

"No—unless perhaps you can find a survey course in philosophical thought. I don't think you'll get what you need in technical courses in either of these fields. The truth is that most of the psychology and philosophy that really helps one to understand man is not found in the textbooks, but in literature. Shakespeare knew more of both fields than all of the professors alive today."

Nancy laughed. "You're probably right. Yes, I like to read, and I like literature and history. I think trying some courses would be fun."

"The idea is to expose yourself to as broad a variety of human experience as possible," I continued. "Only in this way will you find what is there for you. You've already had experiences with a number of different aspects of life, but you have not found your own identity. The next step is to look through the eyes of others, vicariously sharing their experiences in order to absorb whatever may be meaningful to you. Reading and listening to what people have to say will help. And the exercises I give you will stimulate your thinking, as you work to integrate all of these life experiences with your own. This is a process of analyzing the elements that offer something to you, and of synthesizing these into a sense of meaning and purpose that will make your life worthwhile."

So we began the exercises. At first Nancy thought some of them made little sense; others were fun; and to still others she was indifferent. This is the way with most who try them. You can't see where they are leading until you get fairly far along.

These exercises are not cure alls. I would not deceive anyone into believing they are—and they were not for Nancy. There is no simple, easy road to finding a personal identity, but this identity exists for all who are willing to pay the price of persistence in the search.

A few months passed before Nancy began to see where her real hang-up had been, the blocking factor that had kept her from finding permanent satisfaction in any life goal. I could, of course, see it much sooner, but I knew she must discover it for herself.

The answer was elementary: In spite of her lifelong reaction against the establishment, her deepest feelings were quite conventional. And this is true of most who overreact against tradition. She really wanted a stable marriage, children, and a vine-covered cottage. She also needed the additional creative outlet of a cause in whose behalf she could find a unique identity apart from her family.

Many women today feel this double need for the feminine role and the crusader's role. Successful family men have always had dual identities. In the past women identified with their husbands to the extent of sharing vicariously both roles, but in today's age of individuality this identification has grown far less effective.

Nancy did develop plans for the accomplishment of both roles, and she did lose her emotionally charged negativism toward traditional society. She did not lose—or need to—the reaction against hypocritical lip service to traditional values.

She met a physician from another state who worked with the underprivileged. This friendship forged her interest in becoming a graduate social worker. She left the city to begin working toward her graduate degree, and I lost track of her. I can't be certain that she found her purpose in life, but her previous progress suggests that she did.

From this true case of the first writer you can see how it is necessary to look away from your failures and to explore your (often hidden) assets—to **dereflect** your attention from failure to possible sources of success before you can see yourself in a clear enough way to discover the new possibilities for success which you have had within yourself all along but have ignored in concentrating on failures.

When you—male or female—do what Nancy finally got around to doing you will be on the right road.

This brings us to the **exercise** for dereflection, which will help you do what you need to in finding the new meaning and the purposive goals that will fulfill it—the missing elements in your life. You will have looked away from failures and explored previously untapped resources or advantages—assets of which you were unaware, and these will give you the boost you have needed in the direction of success. Do this exercise now (p.233).

Chapter IX

Step 7

The Final Scene: Commitment

Commitment to your new goals in achieving the power of purpose in life.

THE FOLLOWING ILLUSTRATIVE case is from the clinical files of the first writer. All identifying data have been changed to protect the privacy of the individual.

Ralph Easter had been conscientious and effective in applying these exercises of **logoanalysis**. He had worked through an initial period of depression, and had begun to find a new life and to develop the feeling of being Somebody. But when he came to evaluate the changes that had occurred, he found that in spite of a generally progressive picture he had failed in his commitment to new goals. He was hesitant and doubtful about the future. He had made tentative plans, but he did not have self-confidence and faith that they would work. Something was lacking, but he could not find out just what.

He had explored in dilettante fashion almost every kind of life experience, but he could not discover anything that would warrant real dedication. In fact, he appeared to resist his own efforts toward commitment, as if there were a great inner battle between one part of himself that was tired of drifting in life and wanted a definite mission and another part that feared failure of attainment and was afraid to take this chance.

I was growing exasperated with this situation. "When are you going to come out from behind that fence and face life?" I needled him.

"What do you mean, I'm not facing things? You admitted I've been doing well, Doc. why do you set me up and then knock me down? You know I've been trying hard. It's just that I can't keep these nervous spells from coming back every time I settle into a groove, I get some good ideas—you said so, yourself—then I start on them, and then I get shaky. Tranquilizers help some, but not much. So how can I get going in life when I have all these things to face?"

"This is what I mean by hiding behind the fence. You are afraid to accept the risk of failure, so you protect yourself by refusing to play the game."

"Refusing, hell—I try hard to play, but I can't score. That's why I came for help."

"Which means you blame me and everyone but yourself. The truth is, you're at the crossroads in life, but you want someone else to choose the road to take. Nevertheless, only you can exercise this choice for your own life. You get close, and then back away."

"I wish you'd tell me what I could do better."

"All right, maybe I can. Let's look back over your life again, and see if we can work out the hang-up that keeps you from getting started on something."

I surveyed his case history once more. At forty-six he was robust and good looking, stocky in build, with penetrating blue eyes, and a full head of hair, although graying on the sides. A college graduate in business administration, he had worked as an accountant until he had opened his own office as a tax specialist.

He married an attractive, socially inclined girl, who was drawn to his potential as a businessman and community leader.

He took the CPA examination, but failed on the first attempt. He then withdrew into a shell of work and study and spent little time with Arlene and their two small children. She tolerated this at first on the grounds that he would change after he became a CPA, but he found a succession of excuses to avoid taking the examination again, for he could not face the possibility of a second failure.

Family life grew increasingly discordant, and soon became impossible. His wife divorced him. The financial settlement took almost everything he had, and he lost all motivation to try further. His savings were consumed by the divorce trial, and so were his hopes for the future.

He gave up his practice and started drinking heavily. He couldn't keep up his payments for child support, so his ex-wife had him jailed, which sobered him up. The judge let him out of jail upon his promise to get a job and to pay regularly.

He moved to another state, and started over. He got a job, but not in accounting, which he had never liked anyway. His hobby had for some years been amateur photography, and he found a place as floor salesman in a camera shop. It paid poorly, but he enjoyed his work for the first time.

He could not meet the payments to his ex-wife, who tried again to have him jailed; but the courts in his newly adopted state were more lenient. His attorney succeeded in fighting extradition on the other state's contempt of court charge. The original court then agreed to a reduction in the payments. The ex-wife countered by refusing to let him see the children, but he didn't fight this, as he had never felt much like a father anyway.

In time Ralph met another woman who interested him, a widow who continued the operation of her husband's photographic studio. He went to work for her, and within a year they were married. For some years they were happy; they shared a common interest, and worked as well as played together. It seemed that he had found himself.

But again an alienation developed, although he was not able to give any clear reason for it. Neither party had a serious complaint other then incompatibility. This was, however, enough to cause his second wife to sue for divorce. In contrast to the first mate, she was a self-supporting professional, not vindictive, and asked nothing of him but her freedom.

In spite of their drifting apart and his inability to convey his feelings, he was deeply in love with this woman, and the second divorce crushed his spirit. He could not turn to anything connected with photography because of its association with her, and the only escape was a return to drink.

When he hit bottom, he was forced to accept hospitalization as an alcoholic, winding up in a Veterans Administration hospital, for which he was eligible as a World War II serviceman. The VA dried him out, got him back on his feet, and sent him forth, in a somewhat more hopeful state of mind, to conquer his world.

But he failed again, and continued to drift. He managed to stay alive by a succession of jobs, but none held his interest. The same was true of a succession of women friends—or, more accurately, mistresses. He was personable and attractive to the opposite sex, and seemed always to be able to get both a job and a girl when he wanted to. But he had been too badly hurt to risk serious commitment to either. He held several sales and clerical jobs obtained through women friends, but in each case he soon lost interest in both the job and its source.

Periodically he would get back on the bottle, and after an extended binge would end up in one of the VA hospitals for several weeks; and then upon discharge he would start over, always with a new resolution to find a new life goal. But each time he faltered.

When he came to my attention, he had tried all of the

following activities, some of which were occupational, some personal:

1. Accounting.
2. Salesman in a camera shop, a sporting goods store, a shoe store, and a real estate firm.
3. Photographer in his wife's studio.
4. Radio-TV correspondence course—he did not complete this.
5. Alcoholics Anonymous—at first work with this group promised to be his source of identity and purpose, but again he could not stick with it.
6. A leading secret order or lodge. He was initially convinced that here was his mission, but once again the interest did not last. He found little comfort in the idealistic philosophy, which he felt was only verbalized and never practiced by the lodge members.
7. Religion. He returned to the church in which he was reared, one of the major Protestant denominations, and for a time became an active layman. At first he thought he had finally found the answer to his search for meaning in life; but in less than a year he drifted away again, as he had in his teens.
8. An encounter or "T" group. This was one of the new communities of a dozen or so lonesome souls who meet, usually twice weekly, to bare their feelings to each other and to seek mutual acceptance and understanding. Under a professional leader, they try to break down barriers of communication and to build mutual trust. Ralph's group was moderately conservative, not one of the groups that practice nudity.

In the encounter group he felt that he had finally found what he had been seeking. For some months he showed a lot of improvement: He stayed away from alcohol, remained true to the girl he was living with, and even got a job as a bookkeeper, with prospects for good advancement. Accounting was the only field he knew well except photography. Although he loved photography, he could not return to it because of its association with the only woman he had truly loved. He went along well for nearly five months, and appeared to have reorganized his life so that he could accept less than the ideal in both occupation and romance. And this is the kind of situation with which most people end in the practical world.

But no—it was too much to expect Ralph to endure. He had a quarrel with this girl, quit his job, began drinking, and soon returned to the hospital. Again they dried him out and put him on outpatient care.

This was the point at which I picked him up. I was seeing him in outpatient therapy, and I had been working with him for several months. The hospital vocational counseling psychologist had helped him get a clerical job to enable him to support himself until he could work out a plan for a more permanent future life.

As I reviewed all of the facts in his record, he reacted to the obviously repetitive and rather gloomy scene of his existence, in which he had still found no lasting meaning and purpose.

"Guess I'm a pretty sad sack, eh, Doc?"

"Yes, I agree. I don't see any hope for you unless you find something entirely new as a source of meaning in your life."

"That's what you've been saying since I came here, and what I've been trying to do. But this logotherapy isn't helping me. I'm beginning to think it's a lot of crap."

"If you would begin to think, you'd have a chance. Let's take a look at your situation. You have the mental capacity to find a new life for yourself, and you have the abilities necessary to carry out a life goal, and all of the potential for success. You have shown all of this in the way you have done the exercises, and you have repeatedly come up with hopeful ideas for your life. And you have started to follow up these ideas, but every time things begin to look good, you cop out. Hasn't it occurred to you yet that you fail because you don't want the responsibility of success?"

"You're wrong, Doc. You think I like being a nobody, an alcoholic, having nothing? I want the same things in life everybody else does, but I just can't get them."

"What do you want in life?"

"I just want to be happy."

"What is happiness?"

"It's having what you want."

"You're going in circles. What do you want that most people want?"

"Most people—all they want is food, money, and sex."

"So you are like that?"

"I try not to be, but trying is not enough. I wish I could understand what I do want. I try hard, but every time I think I have found the answer, it all turns out to be an illusion, and I'm back to nothing."

"Have you read Somerset Maugham's *The Razor's Edge?*"

"No, but I think I remember a movie about it."

"It is about a man who struggled to find the answers to the basic questions of the meaning of human life. You are going through a lot of the same experiences, and you share many of the same feelings. You should get the book at the library, because it may give you some helpful ideas."

"I'll read it. But I doubt that it has any answers—at least, for me. I've tried so many things, and at first I always think I have found the answer, but it turns out to be only a mirage."

"You've got if figured right, all except *why* everything turns into an illusion. It happens because you have a big fight going on inside yourself. Part of you wants to find a new life, but the other part is afraid of the possibility of failure. You can't accept the responsibility of facing this, so you quit before you have a chance to fail—which also means, of course, that you quit before you have a chance to succeed."

Ralph looked at me hard, and then he looked away. "It doesn't make sense," he said, "I don't understand that at all."

But I felt that he understood. "You have just two choices: To go on as you are, or to do what presently seems to you to be the impossible—to break out of the pattern, find a cause for your existence, and stick to it. Sticking to it will be the hard part; it's the part you've never done. And the reason is that you've never had a reason to go on in spite of discouragement and despair. There is only one kind of reason that will work, namely, an unconditional commitment to the belief that there is an ultimate meaning in all human life, a meaning that makes every life significant—which implies that each life is needed to fulfill a destiny. And if so, this includes you."

"You're dangling religion in my face again, Doc, and that has not worked, not for me."

"It's not religion unless you make it so. It is simply life. You've told me you believe there is a Power beyond that of man, even though you don't like church any more."

"I've tried church, but the people there are a bunch of self-centered phonies. No real love or charity there. Sure, I believe there's a God or *something* to explain this lousy world. But whatever it is, it's a long way off and I can't get close to it, so it doesn't help. You know, Doc" he switched the train of thought in what seemed at first an irrelevant direction, "the thing that has helped me most has been those encounter groups."

Encounter Groups

"You told me that before, and it did seem that you were going to make it while you were in the groups. But in a few months the usual cop-out occurred. Why didn't the groups keep you going?"

"I don't know. Say, Doc, what do you think of encounter and marathon and T-groups and all that?"

"They're just some more gimmicks, like most other forms of therapy; and like the others, they help some people—the people who have faith in them. But you have never been able to maintain consistent faith in anything, especially yourself."

"There's nothing to give a guy faith if you try everything and nothing works out."

"The faith has to come from you and not from the treatment. But your relationship to people can help you build faith. That's why the encounter groups helped. The trouble with a lot of them is that they are artificial relationships set up between people who do not really share any common goals or values in life. The T-groups within the industrial management personnel of a particular company have a common company goal, but your group was a motley mixture of all sorts of people with little to bind them together. The surprising thing is that they work at all under such circumstances. It is not surprising that they have little permanent effect upon the way most people cope with problems of everyday living. To get that effect you have to establish an individual and highly personal relationship, which was the object of our exercise on encounter. And you did pretty well at this; you chose your present girl friend, and the two of you are still together."

"Yes, we love each other, and I think this is going to last."

"She has not yet meant as much to you as did your second wife, but it's up to you to develop this relationship to maturity."

"She goes for this logotherapy; and if it hadn't been for her, I don't think I would have been able to stick out the exercises."

"Does this mean she has a strong faith in something beyond man?"

"Very much so. She senses things that I don't; she's intuitive, like most women are. And she's got a cousin who read some of the stuff, and this girl thinks it's great. I guess women can understand some things about life better than men."

"They're not more intuitive; they just learn to listen more to the intuitive thoughts that come to everybody. But why don't you try an experiment? Why not get the three of you together for an hour or two each week. Form an encounter group. Ask yourselves these questions: How can a person find faith in an ultimate meaning in his own life? What experiences lead people to this faith? What can a person do to find something worthwhile and challenging in an otherwise drab and routine life? Where can he find an identity in a job to be done, a cause to work for? You have been trying for some time to find these answers for yourself, and you have not latched on to anything of sufficient meaning to make the risks of failure and the struggle for success worth taking. Maybe a mutual exchange of ideas on these questions would help to turn up something practical."

"Well—that's a thought. Yes, it might work. I guess we could try it."

Ralph followed through, in response to my prodding. Their first meeting was fun, and broke down into an irrelevant discussion. I pressed him to hold the conversation to the point, and to write down the main thoughts that each expressed. After the first week there was something of a letdown, and I feared that the idea was not working. But at the beginning of the fourth week he reported enthusiastically that he was seeing the point.

"I thought it was a nutty idea at first, and not worth the time. But now I can see what you are getting at—and it works. We've got into the swing of it, and we found two others who are interested in the same thing. This other couple—the man works at the office—came over to our house Friday night. I think they're just living together, like we are. We're all trying to find some answers."

"Are you finding any?"

"I don't know yet. But I've learned one thing: A lot of people are in the same boat. And all the time I felt that I was some sort of freak that had problems nobody else ever faced."

"Yes, that's what most people think of their situations. So one of the values of getting together with others who share a common interest or need is to learn that all kinds of problems fall into patterns. While each person is different, each also shares many similar features with the others."

"It helps to talk things over with the people who feel as lost as you do."

"Certainly. 'Misery loves company' because there is strength in a group, and it adds up to more than the sum of the strengths in each member."

"Well, this is the first time in a long while that I've felt like I might be getting somewhere."

"I'm glad you're getting the feeling. I think you're on the way now. But there's one important caution."

"Caution? What's that?"

"Look for a miracle, but don't expect it."

"What?"

"All life is miraculous and there's a miracle to be found in every life. Often there are many miracles in one life. But frequently, we are so blinded by our hang-ups that we look right at them and can't see them. So it is important not to expect to find the miracles. Then we're not disappointed. They are like happiness—you can't just walk up and capture it. Just as you have to look a little to the side of an object to see it best in twilight, you have to avoid the direct approach to seeing miracles and finding happiness in life."

"I don't get you. What do you mean, avoid trying to find what I'm looking for?"

"I mean, get interested in helping the others to see the miracles in their lives. You'll find this the best way to come upon the miracles in your own life."

Ralph gave me an odd look, and I knew that he would not understand for some time.

Did he finally find the miracle of his life? It depends upon how one views what happened. As a matter of fact, nothing occurred that could be proven in any sense to be a miracle. But something did occur that changed his attitude, and with this came a change in his life. If you had known Ralph, you would concede that changing his attitude required a miracle.

The miracle was that he took my advice. I don't think my giving it had any effect; he took it coincidentally because he stumbled by experience upon the fact that it was sound.

He continued with the group, feeling the frustrations of each member because he had experienced them himself. He more or less accidentally lost himself in helping to figure it all out with them. This role came to be his identity, and it gave his life a sense of purpose. He was the seeker who would help you to search if you didn't know how. This meant that he helped others to find something that he could not find for himself. But this very process operated, without his realizing it, to supply the meaning that he needed in his own life.

At last Ralph had become committed to an attitude that gave life meaning, without his knowing how or when he had done it. He had found something that endured. He had looked to one side of what he was trying to see, and what he sought had been revealed in the action of looking aside. I kept in touch with Ralph for nearly a year after this point, at which time I moved to take a job in another city. At the time I left, he was still maintaining his commitment well. He had stayed off alcohol, which was in itself a major achievement. The key word is **commitment**. He had finally found a value that remained constant and gave him a sense of purpose—he was Somebody.

Now it is your turn to make this same type of commitment in your own life. All of which brings us to the final step in logoanalysis. At this point complete the exercise of Chapter IX Step 7, then return to the final remarks below.

Only you can make yourself persevere in finding the answer and in **commitment** to it. When you feel that you have gained insight into the basic life goals that are right for your future, and that you are ready to pursue them, you will be on the road. From this point on, it is a matter of staying on it and fulfilling the commitment you have made.

A final word of caution: It is always wise to **have more than one goal**, although the goals usually should be related or in the same general family of life meanings. The **reason** is that if one goal should prove unattainable, you can then switch to pursuit of the other without loss of purpose in life. Frankl has pointed out that **despair is the result of one's having placed all**

of his eggs of energy in one basket of meaning; if this is shattered, he is lost and left with an emptiness of purpose. but if you have a "spare to prevent despair" by following the same underlying human need, you can change goals and still travel without interruption on down the same road to self-fulfillment in the attainment of a life mission that will mark you as Somebody.

Now—when you have completed the **commitment exercise** the rest is all up to you. If you have followed the text throughout, and have paralleled it with your answer to the corresponding exercises, you should have developed a new view of your life for the future. It will all be a real challenge. We challenge you to go forth to success. If you feel a snag at any time, review the corresponding chapter and exercise (p.233).

Now as you "graduate" from the seven steps remember that you will have to choose the shape of these relationships and how to handle the bad which you can't avoid. If you have learned the principles in Chapters I and II you will be able to deal with these relationships to your advantage—and you will have learned to do this while avoiding the pitfalls of "raw" sex for its own sake and building instead steps of positive relationships in the Greek sense of love from **erotic** or purely selfish and physical attraction to the power of **agape** or unselfish meaningful intimacy.

If you do you will leave the world a better place than you found it. And that is the highest form of meaning and purpose in life—to count, to make a difference that you lived at all.

If you have had the guts to follow this book, we will bet on you to succeed. We will be happy for you—and for ourselves, because **our success is tied to your success.**

The Identity Exercise

Gaining a Sense of Personal Identity

1. If you had to identify yourself in **one** sentence, what would you say of yourself? Write 5 sentences that would identify you. Start with the one which would furnish the best identity, then the second best, etc.

   _____

   _____

   _____

   _____

   _____

2. Write 5 sentences which you **wish** you could truthfully write to identify yourself.

   _____

3. What keeps you from becoming what you want to be?

The Uniqueness Exercise

How Are You Different From Everyone Else Who Ever Lived?

1. What year were you born? _____
2. Why were you born to live in the present age? Was it pure chance? _____ Or some sort of design or plan in the universe? _____ What are the odds that you would be born during the year of your actual birth by pure chance? _____
3. Where were you born? _____
4. Why were you born there? Was it pure chance? _____ Or some sort of design or plan in the universe? _____
   What are the odds that you would be born in the place where you actually were born by pure chance?
   _____

5. Why were you not born a cave man in prehistoric days?
   _____

   Or an Australian bushman today?
   _____

   Or a medieval peasant in France?
   _____

Or a slave in ancient Egypt?

_____

6. What are the odds that you would have been born *you* by pure chance?

_____

The purpose of this exercise is to reflect upon the characteristics which make all individuals **unique** personalities, different from all others in the history of the world, and therefore worthwhile in their own right. **Your unique** combination of personal experiences gives you a basis for finding the special meaning which only your own life can have. Obviously the actual chance percentages asked can never be known, but are to emphasize that you really are a unique person in the history of the world.

The Role Model Exercise

An exercise which can help you pinpoint just what you really do value in life is the following procedure for selecting the *role models* with whom you can most easily identify:

1. Rate the people listed below on a 10-point scale from 1 (very negative) through 10 (very positive) as to the degree to which you admire them. If you do not recognize a name skip it.

Name	Known for	Rating
Mike Tyson	Boxer	_____
Elizabeth Dole	Politician	_____
Paul the Apostle	Missionary	_____
Diana Ross	Vocalist	_____
Adolph Hitler	German dictator	_____
Martin Luther King, Jr.	Civil rights leader	_____
Dan Rather	TV news anchor	_____
Hillary Clinton	Politician	_____
Rev. Jessie Jackson	Civil rights leader	_____
David Letterman	TV talk show host	_____
Barbara Walters	TV anchor and interviewer	_____
Dr. Jack Kervorkian	Assistant to patients who choose death rather than suffering	_____
J. B. Rhine	Father of modern parapsychology	_____
Diane Sawyer	Talk show host, news anchor	_____
Ernest Hemingway	Author	_____
Saddam Hussein	Iraqi dictator	_____

Cokie Roberts	TV journalist	_____
"Dr. Phil" McGraw	Ph.D. psychologist, counselor on Oprah Winfrey show	_____
Carl Sagan	Astrophysicist	_____
Norman Vincent Peale	Minister, writer	_____
Jennifer Lopez	Actress	_____
Norman Schwartzkopf	Military leader	_____
Emmit Smith	Dallas Cowboys (Football)	_____
Cindy Crawford	Model and actress	_____
Al Gore	Former Vice President	_____
Albert Einstein	Scientist	_____
Elvis Presley	Rock and Roll founder	_____
Peter Jennings	TV news anchor	_____
Oprah Winfrey	TV hostess, actress	_____
Albert Ellis	Ph.D. psychologist, cognitive behavior therapy	_____
Billy Graham	Evangelist	_____
Sarah Jessica Parker	TV star	_____
Colin Powell	Military general, Secretary of State	_____
"Dr. Ruth" Westheimer	Ph.D. sexologist	_____
William Shakespeare	Writer, dramatist	_____
Jerry Falwell	Minister	_____
Princess Diana of Great Britain	Royal family	_____
Mother Teresa	Catholic nun	_____

2. Now list and rate as above ten individuals whom you know (either personally or by reputation) and who have found a cause which has given their lives an obvious meaning and purpose. Note that a cause can be either good or bad in its effect on others.

Name	Known for	Rating
1.		
2.		
3.		
4.		
5.		
6.		

7. _____

8. _____

9. _____

10. _____

Now look over the ratings you have assigned: If you have skipped any names in the first list ignore them and evaluate only the ones you do know. Is there a common thread or factor in the names to which you have assigned high ratings? If so, what? And is there a common thread or factor in the names which you have rated low? If so, what? Write in the space below the life meanings and purposes which both high and low ratings represent. These meanings will reveal the kind of values you hold high and low, and from them you can assess the fundamental or basic type of life goals or activities which will challenge most strongly your best abilities and generate the most powerful motivation to achieve them.

Common factor in low ratings

_____

Common factor in high ratings

_____

Life goals or activities which will best fulfill the meanings reflected in these ratings: (Write down all you can think of right now, but keep these lines open for additions from time to time as you reflect upon this all-important consideration. It is really the culmination of the whole process of discovering new meaning in life.):

_____

The Meaning in Life Evaluation (MILE) Scale

Directions: The following list of twenty values is summarized from answers given by a large sample of individuals who were asked which values they most want in life. You can easily determine which are most important and which are insignificant to you by the following rating technique.

Rate each on a 10-point scale from 10 as most valued to 1 as least valued. Your highest-rated values will be those to emphasize in any life activity; the lowest-rated values will be those to avoid.

You may think that, if you had some of the values, you would automatically have many others. For example, you might feel wealth would bring a number of the others. But rate each value as if it were independent of all others. For example, you might feel that wealth would afford you physical sex, but in comparing the two, assume they are independent. If you could have only one, which would you choose?

Now here are the twenty values to rate:

1. Wealth _____
2. Lasting friendships _____
3. Physical sex _____
4. A good name (high character) _____

5. To be remembered favorably after death _____
6. To gain intimacy _____
7. To be a great leader of people _____
8. Health _____
9. To have power _____
10. To be of great service to people _____
11. To be famous _____
12. To be physically powerful (males) or beautiful (females) _____

13. To be an intellectual _____
14. To find adventure and new experience _____
15. To be happy _____
16. To understand the meaning of life _____
17. To fulfill spiritual goals and obligations _____
18. To have peace of mind _____
19. To gain social acceptance and belonging _____
20. To gain a personal identity _____

After you have rated each value and tabulated the results, there is an important consideration in using them. You might find that you have among your high values No. 15, To be happy, and No. 18, Peace of mind. And you may feel that if you had these, all important others would automatically be included.

Actually it is just the reverse: if you have the things that offer a real meaning in life, happiness and peace of mind will follow as by-products. Logotherapy teaches that happiness and similar goals can never by successfully sought as ends in themselves; they occur only when we cease to concentrate on them and work instead toward a worthwhile purpose that fills our lives with a sense of personal significance and identity. It is only when we transcend ourselves in pursuit of goals that make us valuable to others, that we really sense our own self-value and personal worth in a way that produces the warm glow of happiness and peace of mind.

So if you have fallen into the trap of placing too high a priority on happiness and other values of personal satisfaction as goals to be sought in themselves, now is the time to rethink your way through the real meaning of your life and to zero in on those values that can truly work in the quest for happiness—those values that are in and of themselves aimed, not at your own happiness, but rather at the happiness of others who are significant in your life. In your **rating** of happiness and peace of mind, however, record what you would have felt before reading the above statement.

After making all ratings, look at the five highest and the five lowest ratings. Is there a common thread in each group? This thread will show you the type of value you consider most important and the type you think are least important.

Is this the value system you consciously feel is most important to you? If not, consider how to change the values to fit what you really want to pursue in life.

Choosing Your View of Life

Note: The material for this exercise is textual in nature and overlaps considerably with similar material in Chapter 3 of the book. It is given here because there is considerable added data and it is presented in a different context.

When you read this exercise's text, choose one of the three conclusions: view 1, view 2, or view 3 (In between the others).

The *first step* in applying logoanalysis is choosing a basic approach to the question of life meaning. Throughout the entire recorded history of the human race there have been two—and only two—basic attitudes of man toward himself. We find these in ancient Egyptian cultures, in Hebrew life at the time of Christ, and in the America of the last part of the twentieth century. And after five thousand years of recorded history, there is no more accurate way of settling the issue of which one is correct, there is no more proof of the validity of either, than there was in the beginning. So you have to make your own evaluation and choose the view that seems most reasonable to you.

Which you choose does make an important difference, because your choice will determine *how* you are going to proceed in the search for life meaning. And it is important that you do make a choice and not try to evade the question, for those who take the latter course—and they include a large segment of the human race—never really find a true meaning and purpose in life. This is because any genuine meaning stems from one or the other of the two views.

Your curiosity is no doubt by this time sufficiently whetted concerning just what the two approaches could be, although you would probably be able to deduce them for yourself if you tried. Here they are:

1. Man is merely a machine, a mechanical device; his biological organism follows the mechanical laws of nature as do all other aspects of nature, and he is nothing more than any other organism—such as a rat or a cat—except that he is more complex. All of nature is the result of chance factors; in spite of the regularities of natural laws, there is no purpose and meaning behind it. Of course this view would logically hold that there is no afterlife or survival of personality after death.

This is the view of so-called positivistic science, the view of "mechanism," the "reductionist" view which holds that all of man's psychological processes can be reduced to physical processes, the view of "determinism," which considers all mental and physical events to be caused or determined by physical antecedents.

This mechanistic view says that there is no intrinsic meaning or purpose in life. Man's only chance for meaningful living is based on what he can devise for himself. He must lift himself by his own bootstraps, because there is no external help for him from any "Higher Power." Some, including the famous Harvard behaviorist psychologist B. F. Skinner, would even deny that man can do anything for himself, since, they believe, life is entirely determined by external forces.

The mechanistic view of man is in many respects illustrated by the philosophy of the late French existentialist Jean-Paul Sartre.

Sartre was the leader of atheistic existentialism. Existentialism, which also has a theistic branch, holds that the focus of the study of man should be on his existence as a human being. And both branches hold that human life cannot be understood by reason alone, and that man has freedom of choice as to how he will face life.

But Sartre believed that there is no meaning and purpose in the universe other than what each human individual can put there for himself. All life is *absurd* (a technical term in existentialism that means, not that life is ridiculous, but that it cannot be comprehended by reason). We are all doomed to defeat in the end, according to Sartre, for there is no justice in nature. But in spite of this, we can each find some values in which we believe, and we can live by these values to the last. And living thus—superimposing our own meanings on a meaningless world—enables us to be superior to the absurdity of it all and to die with dignity in the knowledge that we created our own meaning where there really is none. All of this makes life worth living, as Sartre saw it.

Yes, this is the world of Jean-Paul Sartre, and positivistic scientists have a similar view, although they differ on such matters as freedom of the will and deny the existence of freedom. This is the world of most behavioral scientists today, especially most psychologists. The majority of psychologists consider themselves behaviorists, holding that only behavior, and not subjective experience (or conscious experience), is admissible "evidence" in the study of man.

This is one of the two basic views of nature. It is the majority view in scientific circles today, but it is as old as the hills; it is not something new from the modern laboratory.

There is another view, which also has always been with us:

2. Man is a machine, but he is also infinitely more than a machine. His psychological processes, conscious experience, emotions, and feelings do involve processes in the brain and in the rest of the nervous system and the body, but they cannot be reduced to bodily processes. This snag of reductionism (in psychology it is called the psycho-physical axiom) has long been a thorn in the side of scientists who are also religious: It has seemed to them that it knocks out any possibility of spiritual

phenomena. But the work of mathematical physicist Frank Tipler demonstrates all psychological processes; but it is our incomplete knowledge of physical laws that makes them **seem** "supernatural." Tipler believes in immortality and demonstrates how it can be accomplished physically. (See Tipler, Frank. **The Physics of Immortality**, 1994.) Failure to recognize Tipler's point has probably done more than anything else to cause people who would like to reject the mechanistic view of life to be in conflict between the two while usually supporting mechanism because it is "scientific." Tipler shows that this division is apparent but not real, and that in reality there is no conflict between true science and true religion.

This second non-mechanistic view is called the "teleological" view (from Greek *teleos*, goal or end); it holds that there is a purpose in the universe and in all life, but that only human kind can, as philosopher Max Scheler said, "contemplate the possible" that is, what can and should be.

The dog accepts nature as is and has no concept of a better world; but human beings can conceive of a whole new way of life and can work toward its attainment. They are not limited by the past or even the present; they can control their future.

This view holds that the universe is not merely the product of chance but is designed by an Intelligence greater than any we know. It considers us as a part of this design and therefore believes that we have our own unique meaning and purpose: We all have a destiny to fulfill, a life purpose to carry out.

Each of us must search for it; but when we become convinced that we have discovered it, we have a real mission to fulfill, a cause to work for, a task to complete in life that will motivate us to such a powerful degree that we can go on. We will continue in spite of life's frustrations and make it through or over or under or around obstacles because we have a reason that makes it all worth the struggle.

This view would logically hold that there is some sort of afterlife or persistence of personality after bodily death, although there are those who embrace the view without believing in survival. This nonmechanistic orientation rejects determinism and holds that we are all free within the limits set by heredity and environment to choose how we will face our situation. As Frankl says, life conditions are given to us; how we face them is freely chosen by us.

This is the world of the religious person, but it is also the world of many who do not think of themselves as religious—of many who would certainly not be religious in the institutional sense, in the sense of organized religion, in the "church" sense, but who do believe in a Power greater than man, and who have their own personal ways of contacting this Power. Alcoholics Anonymous is based on this approach, in which each individual defines his own concept of this Power but still turns to it for help.

This is the world of those who believe that there is a Power toward which man can turn for help, whether he does it by religion in the conventional sense or by his own methods. It is a world of purpose and design in which each individual life counts, in which we make our lives count in spite of whatever setbacks and tragedies and frustrations we face. We do this by looking for the hidden meaning in it all, for the way in which all of our life events fit into a pattern and point to a purpose we can fulfill, to a meaning we would not have been able to realize if these problems had not occurred.

This is the *attitudinal value* in logotherapy, described in the last chapter and illustrated by the case of the eighty-year-old woman with terminal cancer, whom Frankl treated. The attitudinal value can be applied by those who follow the mechanistic view of man, by their asking themselves what they can do to turn their rotten luck into some advantage; but it is much more easily applied by nonmechanistic believers in an intrinsic purpose in all of nature, for they do not have to consider their conditions as "rotten luck." They rather think of these conditions as part of a purpose that is to be discovered and fulfilled.

This second, nonmechanistic holds that there is a plan or design in nature toward which natural events are moving. For most people this view is not only a more optimistic attitude toward life, but also a helpful and needed source of courage when the going in life gets tough. Most people's teeth are not sharp enough and their fingernails are not long enough to go it alone in the human jungle that they often find themselves facing. But for some, like Jean-Paul Sartre and psychologist-sexologist Albert Ellis, this attitude represents a failure of the individual to take responsibility for life upon his own shoulders and to handle this situation without "magical" help (which these authorities believe does not exist in the first place, and which they say they do not want in the second place).

Well, which of the two views of man is right? The truth is that leading spokesmen for both points of view agree that neither view can be proven in the scientific sense. Both are in the last analysis a matter of faith. Many religious persons have a deep and abiding faith that there is a Creator who has a specific plan for their lives. Many like Sartre have a faith that there is not. Sartre says that he intuitively knows there is no God, just as Billy Graham would say that he intuitively knows there is one.

All of this leads many to try to avoid the issue altogether until they reach some life crisis when they need to come to grips with it and to have a faith upon which they can base action. The trouble with such procrastination is that, if you wait until you need a faith, you won't be able to establish it overnight. Whichever way your faith may turn, it has to jell and become a genuine part of you. And until you have a firm decision that fits your personal needs, you won't have a real peace of mind.

People are emotionally different in their needs to believe in these two views of the nature of man. You will be able to find a real meaning and purpose in life from either view *if* (1) you *really* believe in it, and (2) you are *emotionally suited* to believe in and to accept this view. The latter factor hangs many people up today. They are trying in this increasingly secular society to believe in, or to live as if they believed in, the mechanistic view that there is no purposeful design in the universe placed there by some Creator. They consider the teleological view mystical, supernatural, and fairy-tale-like, and they want no part of it—until they meet a life situation in which they discover that they are not the superstrong stainless steel independent types they thought they were, and that they really do need some help. Then it is too late to get the help, because their doubts of a purposeful universe have become so firmly ingrained that they cannot readily perceive the world in meaningful terms.

This point is well illustrated by a patient in one of our logotherapy groups in an alcoholic rehabilitation program several years ago. Believe it or not, he was a large-city psychiatrist. When we came to study the present topic, he was deeply moved.

"Doctor," he said, "I am here in the hospital because I cannot resolve this problem in my own mind. I know that's why I drink. I have the emotional need to believe that there is a meaning and purpose in the universe, put there by a Creator who cares about me and will help me fulfill that purpose if I turn to him and seek to find it. But when I try, I am beset with doubts, and I can't stick to either view. I tolerate it as long as I can, and then I grab a bottle."

"Doctor," I returned, "you are not alone in this struggle. There is no proof, but there *is* a lot of evidence. There is evidence on both sides, and each side is convincing to many people who are suited for it. If you will really take the time and energy to search for the evidence on the side you need to believe in, you will find it. And only then will you find yourself."

He went through a long struggle that discouraged him, and he left the hospital without finding himself. But within a year, he had come to grips with the question well enough to get back into practice. When he finds others fighting this battle, he will know how they feel and will probably be better able to help than would a psychiatrist to whom the problem has no personal significance.

For those like him who need to believe in a Higher Power but haven't found satisfactory evidence, the following facts may help:

1. Scientists are losing their sense of intellectual superiority, according to Richard Olson of the University of California at Santa Cruz, writing in *Psychology Today*, January 1976. He notes that certain developments within the sciences, such as the Heisenberg Indeterminacy or Uncertainty Principle, have indicated that there are some physical events that cannot be predicted by natural laws. This leaves the whole field of science vulnerable to critics who have always said that science could never attain absolute knowledge, as noted in the "Press Digest" of *Current Contents* for April 5, 1976. All of which opens the door to the belief that there are some things that cannot be explained by the concept of a mechanistic universe devoid of purpose and design.

2. Elizabeth Kübler-Ross, M.D., whose book *On Death and Dying* (1969) is perhaps the best-known work concerning the terminally ill, has for many years been collecting reports of a large number of individuals who were pronounced medically dead but who later were resuscitated, and who retained memories of this period during which they were supposedly dead. *Reader's Digest* (August 1976) reports interviews with Dr. Kübler-Ross for *Family Circle* and *People* magazines, in which she talked of her conclusions from her studies. She had before then doubted there is any life after death, but changed her mind firmly afterward. She feels that something significant happens within minutes after "clinical" death, as her patients became amazingly peaceful in expression at that time.

Kübler-Ross investigated scores of patients, both religious and nonreligious, some of whom had been "dead" for three to twelve hours. Most reported one basic type of experience: they felt as if they had shed their physical bodies, and they experienced peace, freedom from pain and anxiety, and a sense of completeness or perfection. Some could "see" the efforts to revive them, and they resented attempts to return them to a life of suffering. None were afraid to die again.

In February 1977, it was the first writer's privilege to participate in a Festival of Meaning honoring Dr. Viktor Frankl, the founder of logotherapy, organized by Dr. Robert Leslie of the Pacific School of Religion in Berkeley, California, upon the occasion of the establishment there of the Frankl Library and Memorabilia. At a dinner for Dr. Frankl, the famous Viennese psychiatrist mentioned that Dr. Kübler-Ross had recently come to see him. We asked him how he had reacted to her collection of cases. He pointed out that, because the concepts of time and space are human psychological constructs and have meaning only in the world of human experience, it is really not valid to think in terms of events after death or before life. This means that, in a sense apart from the human experience of the sequence of events which we consider as time and of the distances which we know as space, the concepts of past, present and future blend, and the meanings of "here" versus "there" merge. Thus life becomes a continuous process (even though it changes in form of expression) without beginning or end. Following the evidence produced by Kübler-Ross, and the reminder of the relative nature of the time-space continua noted by Frankl, one might conclude that it is a basic mistake on man's part to interpret birth-life-death sequences in terms of beginning and end; they are rather episodes in universal experience that transcends·time and space. Frankl holds that no experience, once it occurs, can ever be lost—it remains always as an occurrence in nature regardless of all other events that may transpire. (See Frankl's book, *The Unheard Cry for Meaning: Psychotherapy and Humanism*, New York: Simon and Schuster, 1978; specifically the chapter, "Temporality and Morality.")

The sum of these facts suggests that life cannot be adequately viewed as an accidental flash in a meaningless universe of absurdity and chaos, but that it is part of a continuing, dynamic, unfolding process. And how can such a process, which is by definition not "chance determined" and chaotic, occur without some kind of Power or Intelligence in the universe to determine or ordain it?

As Martin Heidegger, the great German existentialist philosopher, has said, "The existential question [the question of the meaning of existence] is not, Why is this or that here? The real existential question is, Why is there something instead of nothing at all?"

Winston Churchill said to the United States Congress on December 26, 1941, shortly after America's entry into World War II, "I will say that any man must have a blind soul who cannot see that some great purpose and design is being worked out here below." Eugene A. Cernan, Apollo 17 astronaut, said (*The Plain Truth*, June 1976), "When you get out there a quarter of a million miles from home, you look at Earth with a little different perspective . . . The Earth looks so perfect. There are no strings to hold it up . . . You think of the infinity of space and time. I didn't see God but I am convinced of God by the order out in space. I know it didn't happen by accident."

3. The biggest barrier to belief in a High Power for many is the sense of thwarted justice that seems to pervade human life. If there were a Higher Power, why would He (or It—or She, in deference to Women's Lib) permit such horrendous circumstances to occur? And when they occur to us, our natural first reaction is, Why me? The answer to this question is crucial in our capacity to find any real meaning and purpose in our lives.

Those whose answer is, It is my rotten luck—the result of "pure chance" in a meaningless universe—must then, in order to find any personal life meaning in this meaningless world, ask themselves the further questions: What can I do on my own, lifting myself by my own bootstraps, since there is no external help, to turn my misfortunes to my own advantage? How can I use them constructively to create a meaning where none now seems to exist in nature? Persons who reason thus must accept responsibility to create such a meaning or perish in despair.

On the other hand, those whose answer to the first question is, These misfortunes and injustices do not seem to make any sense, but I accept them as a part of a plan or design in nature, as a part of the design for my own life, as having a purpose that I cannot see, even though it appears so horribly unjust—those whose answer is along these lines must next ask themselves, What could this purpose be?

Now their third question will be the same as that of those who believe the universe is meaningless and the result of pure chance: What can I now do to use my misfortunes constructively, to turn my suffering to advantage by finding something worthwhile to do that I could not have done so well if these tragedies had not occurred? You may wonder, therefore, what difference it makes whether we believe the universe is chaotic or designed. But there is a big difference here: The "design people" don't have to say, What rotten breaks, but I'll lift myself by my own bootstraps and go on anyway, even though it is very hard to keep up courage in such a terrible world. They instead say, My experiences have been terrible, but they have a purpose that I am supposed to fulfill through having had them; therefore I will search for this purpose, I will try to see what these experiences could be intended to teach me or in what direction they could be leading me. I will choose the positive attitude that such purpose exists, and I will search for it. And in the search I can expect help: I do not have to depend solely on my own strength in a world that is too much for any person; I can look to this Higher Power that has ordained the purpose I cannot see, and I can expect guidance in the search and assistance when I falter.

A strong point regarding this matter of dealing with a frustrated sense of justice in an unjust world was often made by

Frankl: he asked, Do you suppose that an animal in a laboratory experiment can understand the meaning of its suffering? Can it comprehend the fact that this unpleasantness serves a purpose higher than any that its limitations permit it to grasp? In the same way, is it not possible that man experiences suffering that has a purpose higher than any that his own limitations permit him to see?

In this connection, an incident in the senior writer's experience may illustrate what Frankl is talking about, as he deals with this difficulty most people have in maintaining faith and courage in the face of the ubiquitous occurrence of grossly unjust and unexpected human suffering:

> One evening I had just returned from church, where the preacher's homily had included the statement that, when he was in seminary, his brother, who was also expecting to become a priest, drowned. His first reaction to the tragedy was to withdraw from seminary. Why should he serve such an unjust God? Fortunately his mother's influence in facing the situation with courage and faith finally turned his own tide and enabled him to go on.
>
> As I returned home with this sermon in mind, I had to step over a freshly painted doorstep to enter our condominium. Our next-door neighbor was outside, and I was suddenly greeted by her dog, whom I had often petted. But now I had to halt the dog's advance upon the fresh paint by a sharp rejecting attitude. The neighbor, seeing what was happening, cuffed the dog sharply, and he yelped in retreat.
>
> I wondered how the dog would react to me when I next saw him, how he would make sense of the fact that one day I petted him and the next rejected him for no apparent reason, and then after that attempted to pet him again. How do you explain to a dog that it was

necessary to hurt him in order to prevent greater injury (in this case, getting his paws full of poisonous lead paint, which he undoubtedly would have tried to lick off; as well as his unknowingly injuring others through ruining the paint job)?

How do you explain to a dog the reason for events that are beyond his world of experience and therefore his comprehension? How does God explain to a man?

No, the dog didn't understand; but when I next saw him, he wagged his tail in friendship. He had accepted me on faith, based on the good experiences of the past and is spite of the bad. He wasn't bitter about what he couldn't comprehend. Sometimes dogs are smarter than people.

4. The question of whether the universe is designed and purposeful and of whether there is a Higher Power that made it so are related, as we have seen, to the question of personal survival after death. The latter issue may be better understood by consideration of the fact that personal survival *before* death does not actually occur. That is to say, we do not maintain the same identity throughout life, even though there is a degree of continuity.

This concept is well known in the metamorphosis of some insects, wherein, for example, a caterpillar changes into a moth; but we usually do not associate such a process with human life. And yet in the human organism an analogous process does take place. As we grow from infancy to childhood to adulthood to old age, we go through both physical and mental stages between which there is a thread of continuity based on remembered experience and habits of behavior, but which are separated by differences in appearance, thinking, and behavior that are really more distinct from each other than the differences between individuals at a given period of life. If you are over forty, you are in many respects more like your contemporary friends than you are like yourself at the age of eighteen.

Thus we do not survive this life unchanged; we do not really survive as the same person. We can therefore hardly expect to survive the transition of death unchanged, though the latter may be seen as a *sudden* transition in comparison with the *slow* transition from youth to old age. But here again, since time and space are concepts based on the experience of this life, experience apart from it may not reflect this same sense of time difference. Survival may therefore occur without involving the rigid continuation of form and matter in the frame of reference of time and space to which we are accustomed. And this survival may be based on purpose and design in a meaningful universe, in which we can look to a Higher Power for guidance and help.

5. Evidence that the universe is not a mere mechanism as conceived by materialistic science, but that there are "nonmechanistic" laws yet unknown in nature (which open the door for the concepts of design and purpose in the universe, and for the existence of a Higher Intelligence) is abundant in the field of *parapsychology*. Formerly called psychic phenomena, the occurrences studied in this field include psychokinesis ("mind-over-matter" manifestations), appearances and disappearances that seem to defy the known laws of natural science, mental telepathy and clairvoyance (named ESP or extrasensory perception by Dr. J. B. Rhine at Duke University), and various other related effects.

They are now known as *psi* phenomena. Although many skeptics still exist, the study of these phenomena has considerable scientific acceptance today, as witnessed by the fact that there is a division of parapsychology in the American Association for the Advancement of Science, whereas parapsychologists could not have gotten through the *back* door of this august body a generation ago.

It is true that the parapsychologists (so called because the "orthodox" psychologists considered them outside of respectable psychology in the early years: Greek *para* means beyond, outside) have not yet produced a truly "repeatable" laboratory experiment. This means one that can be duplicated in virtually any scientific laboratory at will with essentially the same results; and we personally hold out for this criterion as essential, because it has been a cornerstone of proof in all *experimental* sciences. But the evidence for psi phenomena has continually grown stronger over the last forty years.

There is voluminous literature on the subject, which you may find at any good library. The laboratory work is essential to proof, but it grows out of the vast background of frequently reported human experiences that seem to involve such phenomena. The first writer has recorded some of these occurrences in Chapter 3 of his book, *Everything to Gain: A Guide to Self-Fulfillment through Logoanalysis* (see Bibliography). We will give only two examples here, since you can find an abundance of them in literature. In fact, you very well may have some such experience to add yourself; and if you do not, the chances are excellent that someone close to you does have.

A lady told us this story:

"The strangest event of my life occurred on the evening of February 23, 1965. I kept saying that it was not my voice, and yet it had to be. There was no one else around except my escort, who was standing just behind me, ready to open the car door. 'Did you say that?' he asked. 'Did you say, "Don't go down Averill Street"? It didn't sound like you.' 'I—I don't know—it wasn't my voice,' I faltered.

"Actually Averill Street was the closest route to my home from the supper club where we had just finished a quiet meal. At the time I had just begun to recover from a very serious illness and had not been out of the house for two months. My friends had all tried to help in the recovery, and Sam, my escort, whom I had known only as a good friend of my late husband's, took me out for an evening of 'real food and fine music for a change.'

"I had gone against my better judgment, because I had felt apprehensive for no apparent reason. As we now pulled out of the parking lot, Sam said, 'Teresa, I see no reason why we can't go down Averill Street. Do you know of any reason why we shouldn't?' 'No,' I replied, 'I don't know why I said that. It's not my nature to back-seat drive. It just didn't seem like I said it, but I must have. No, Sam, of course there is no reason why we can't go down Averill Street.'

"So we went down Averill. And only several minutes later we were hit broadside on my side of the car by another automobile. The car was totaled, and I suffered a crushed side and permanent nerve damage to my right arm. Sam was not injured.

"When he was allowed to see me in the hospital, his first words were, 'How in the hell did you know we should not have gone down Averill Street?' 'I don't know,' I managed to mumble. 'It just wasn't my voice. And don't blame yourself, because I was warned, and I disregarded the warning.' Even today, on the occasions when my right arm gives me fits, I think back to that strange occurrence and wonder what really happened."

What do you think happened?

The same lady very recently told us another story:

"The air was cold and damp this morning [December 1976], and I wore a head scarf as I drove alone to church, even though head gear is seldom necessary here on the Gulf Coast. As I approached to within two blocks of the church, it felt as though someone in the back seat behind me had suddenly plucked the scarf off of my head. I looked around as best I could while driving, and of course there was no one else in the car, and I could not see the scarf. All of the doors and windows were tightly closed because of the cold weather.

"When I parked the car I began to search for the scarf, but it was nowhere to be found. Thinking it might fall out as I opened the door, I watched closely, and then I searched all around the car and thoroughly in the back, under the seats, and everywhere, but nothing!"

The following morning the lady had her husband vacuum the car and make a thorough search, but nothing was found.

"I simply couldn't believe it," she said, "but my sense of humor finally came through, and I said to myself, 'If I'd known the spooks needed a scarf so badly, I'd have worn a brand new one, and not my old favorite.'"

Well, what do you think happened in this case? Is the lady lying? Are these events hoaxes? Coincidences? Hallucinations? Is the lady crazy?

We don't think so. She has never shown any special interest in parapsychology, spiritualism, mysticism, or any form of the occult. She is a devout believer in institutional religion, and she has always accepted the existence of a world beyond man's understanding on the basis of a firm but uncomplicated faith, without attempts to rationalize it or to probe its nature. She has never been known to center her thoughts on manifestations of the nonmaterial world, because she has never needed these to bolster her faith.

These manifestations are, however, very abundant in the literature of parapsychology. Now if you are a hard-core mechanist, you will assume such things are impossible, and that people who report them must by lying, crazy, self-deceived, the victims of hoax or coincidence. If you have already determined not to believe, no amount of evidence—not even that of your own eyes—will convince you. But if you have an open mind, you will do a lot of wondering about reports of this type.

And you may find in parapsychology what you need as a basis for a reasonable faith that there is more to the universe than mechanistic science allows. Here you may gain encouraging evidence that there is, after all, some sort of purpose and design in nature, and that behind it exists a designing Power.

6. In conceiving the question of design in the universe, it may help to draw an analogy between what you have to do in interpreting this universe and what you do in perceiving the

ambiguous stimuli provided by "projective techniques" in clinical psychology. The best known of these techniques is the Rorschach Ink Blot Test, a series of ten supposedly meaningless ink blots which are variously seen by different people as everything and as nothing under the canopy of heaven. Your personal interpretation will depend upon your unique background of individual experience, although there are common patterns or "popular responses."

Now are these blots the result of "pure chance" or of purpose and design? From one standpoint, they are pure chance, since they were made by pouring ink upon paper with a middle crease and then folding the paper upon the crease and thus smearing the ink. But on the other hand, Hermann Rorschach, the Swiss psychiatrist who invented them, made some ten thousand blots before he got a final ten that elicit the maximal number and variety of responses. So from another standpoint, the blots represent an element of purpose and design superimposed upon the pure chance factors that shaped them.

The late great philosopher Alfred North Whitehead believed that something like this occurs in the world of nature: most events are determined by chance; but every so often, at key points (which Whitehead called "occasions") in a person's life, nonchance factors—the result of purpose and design put there by a Higher Power—do occur.

From this point of view, the universe is sometimes mechanistic and chance determined and sometimes teleological and purposive. To represent a similar kind of comparison, the philosopher Herbert Spencer used an analogy with a curved lens or mirror: from one side it is concave, from the other it is convex. Both interpretations are true, depending upon the viewing position.

From this analogy, it might seem that we could "straddle the fence" by accepting both views of the nature of the world and of man, and thus avoid a choice or decision between them. But here it should be noted that, in order to use the mirror, we must decide the effect we want, for the image is different from each point of view. So we really do have to decide what we think about life before we can find a meaning in it.

7. In the last analysis, the strongest line of evidence as to whether there is a Higher Power comes from our individual personal experience. This is always the most convincing argument. The late Dr. Martial Boudreaux, a psychiatrist whom we shall be quoting presently in connection with evidence for the mechanistic view of the universe, said that he has no religious sentiments, but that the nearest thing to them for him is the moving response he sometimes had to music. This shows that he has correctly identified religion as a personal emotional experience, although he has shut off such experience in his own life.

A psychologist friend, who had been religious and then lost her religious faith, told us that she missed nothing about religion except a sense of Presence—the feeling that someone was always with her, which she had once had. This indicates that religion is not social but personal in essence; and belief in the existence of this sense of Presence or Higher Power is determined, not by reason, but by factors of personal experience, which are primarily related to feelings and emotions.

So the best indicator of what your own position should be on this issue is not your head but your heart. If you have the heart for either of the two views, you will put your head to work in finding supportive evidence for it. And there is plenty for each view, although, as we have said, there is no scientific proof of either.

All of which reflects the point being herein made, that the really convincing evidence of the existence of a Higher Power comes, for those who find it, from within rather than from without: it stems from personal experience. There are many, even clergymen, who have never had personal experiences that yield a sense of the presence of this Power, but who believe it is there. For many others, only this personal type of experience is convincing.

Now what about the other side of the coin? To return to the mechanistic view, what lines of evidence are there for those who do not experience a need to believe in this Power, who really show no emotional need for it, and who prefer, like Jean-Paul Sartre, to go through life alone without expecting any outside help? What evidence is there that there is *not* such a Power?

The truth is that, since there is no universal negative, and the existence of such a Power can never be scientifically disproven any more than it can be proven, the negative evidence is, as we have seen, also a matter of faith. But what facts support this kind of faith?

Actually this negative view is based primarily on the assumption that, if there were such a Power, it would be possible to demonstrate the fact scientifically—an assumption that cannot be supported in logic any more than the assumption that the absence of such a Power should be provable scientifically. So we must choose our direction here on the basis of which way life experience leads.

This fact is well illustrated through the opinions expressed by a psychiatrist to whom we already referred, the late Dr. Martial Boudreaux, a psychiatrist who was on the staff of the Gulfport, Mississippi, Veterans Hospital. Here is what he said:

> 'I opt for the mechanistic or chance viewpoint. The nature of basic physical and chemical organization determines the future over eons of time. How this basic organization came about or if it is universal I have no idea, and could not care less . . . My evidence is based on the sum total of my experience, and it represents the way I have thought since early youth. It includes the sum total of all of my reading and personal conversations with people of all types. I do not consider either view capable of proof, and I do not find this disconcerting. So you take your choice and go with it. Years ago

arguments mattered to me; now I don't care. Both sides are incapable of proof, and both are capable of some refutation . . . As far as the need for a meaning and purpose in the universe is concerned, I can hack it successfully without one. But each person has to have his own way and to go with it.'

We think there is little that can be added to these statements in representation of the basic mechanistic orientation toward human life. While a large number of people, especially those who are strongly religious on the one hand or strongly antireligious on the other, become quite emotionally biased in their arguments, this psychiatrist maintained an objective attitude toward both views while choosing one attitude for himself. And that is all we can ask of ourselves or of anyone else.

The key to making a personal decision concerning which of these two basic philosophies of life to adopt lies in one's level of personal self-confidence. If you are self-confident, you will trust your ability to make the right decision. Knowing you can't prove either and that the choice must be made on faith, you will—if you lack faith in yourself—also lack faith in your choice. On the other hand, believing in yourself will mean that you will believe in your choice, even though it is made in the face of incomplete data. To have faith in anything, we must first have faith in ourselves. That is why we will be dealing with ways to build self-confidence in another chapter.

Chapter V

Step 3

Self-Confidence

Developing Self-Confidence in Facing Both Sexes

WE CALL THIS the **Power of Freedom Exercise** because it is based on the fundamental assumption that man does have an area of free will, that all human life is *not* completely determined by conditioning plus heredity, and that therefore we can exercise some free choices to modify our own situation and to direct our lives toward chosen goals. This fundamental belief in freedom is essential to our building self-confidence and to developing creative thinking—indeed, to the entire process of finding life meaning.

You may have "bought" this viewpoint by this time. In case you haven't, there is much evidence we can offer.

B. F. Skinner, the famous Harvard psychologist, believed that we have no freedom of the will, that we are only pawns pushed about by influences of heredity and environment, and that our behavior is all conditioned by external forces—like the behavior of the rats he trains in his "Skinner boxes." Viktor E. Frankl, the famous founder of logotherapy, said that, in spite of the conditions set by heredity and environment, we are free to choose the attitude we will adopt in facing our life situations. Let's see who is right.

1. If you can control your will, you are free. (This is simply the definition of what it means to be free.)
2. If you can will to perform—or not to perform—a given act, you can control your will.
3. If you can throw "odd man out" at will, you can will to perform—or not to perform—a given act.

So—can you throw "odd man out" at will? You may have played the group game of pooling some reward, then throwing down one or two fingers at will, so that the person who throws differently from the others drops out, until only two are left to split the reward. Can you really throw down one or two fingers at will? If so, you have freedom of the will. Test it as follows:

Get a friend to command in advance how you should throw your fingers (one or two). First obey his commands. Then throw opposite to his commands. Can you switch from obedience to defiance at will? If so, you have demonstrated your freedom. I know from experience that every normal person can do so. The only exceptions are people who are severely brain-damaged or who have lost control over their muscles.

This demonstration will have shown that you have will power at your command. If you are religious, you may think of it as God Power, Divine Power, the power of God in man. If you are not religious, you might call it Personal Power. In either case it is *available* Power, the power of will, the power to make choices. With Power comes responsibility—your responsibility to use it to help yourself.

In order to use this Power within, you must release it from the "deep freeze" in which most of us find our potential Power due to disuse. We can release it only by drawing it into activity. The Power of Freedom Exercise can bring your Power into use.

1. Repeat aloud or to yourself a *thematic priming meditation* such as the Ave Maria, the Lord's Prayer, a Yoga Matra, the Sh'ma Yisrael, or the like. If you are not religious, an excellent priming meditation is the Serenity Prayer of Alcoholics Anonymous: "Give me the power to change that which can and should be changed, the serenity to endure that which must be endured, and the wisdom to know the one from the other." Even though this is called a prayer, it may also be used as simply a meditative wish.

2. For the first three minutes of the eight-minute session, build *self-confidence* by autosuggestion: repeat aloud or to yourself the following sentences:

"I am gaining self-confidence, because I am worthy of success. I will succeed. I will succeed because I cannot fail with the Power within on my side. I have the same creative Power within me that is in all people. The Power is greater than any person, but present in all people. I will hereby employ it to strengthen, guide, and sustain me." Say these sentences over and over for a full three minutes.

Now at first you will think this is a lie. At first it will be a lie, but it is a "good" lie. A good lie is one that is both harmless and helpful. If you tell good lies often enough, you will believe them yourself. And the moment you believe them yourself, they cease to be lies and become true. This is brainwashing, but it is the "good kind," that is, the kind you do yourself for your own benefit. You have a right to wash your own brain anytime you want to. You are choosing to do this exercise of your own free will, and that is quite different from having someone else brainwash you by forcing you to say aloud what they want you to believe.

3. During the remaining five minutes, think of the problem area with which you most need help now. Then let you mind relax and "fire at will"—that is, think of what it wants to. Take

notes on ideas that pop into your mind, and keep a log of these ideas. Watch for meaningful patterns in them.

During this five-minute period, do your best to "let you mind go blank." You will find that all sorts of thought will pop up to fill the blank period. This is similar to the free association of psychoanalysis.

At first, the thoughts may be mostly negative—fears, resentment of injustice, etc. This is to be expected. *If negative thoughts become too intense, you can knock them out* by returning to *autosuggestion* and repeating several times the affirmations in it. This may be necessary over a period of some days. It is based on the psychological principle that, while you can think of more than one thing at a time, you cannot concentrate on more than one thing. So forcing yourself to concentrate on the positive knocks out the negative.

Soon you will find that the negative thoughts and feelings are subsiding and that positive material is beginning to come into your mind. Often, however, this will happen at times other than during the five-minute meditation period—at times when you least expect it, perhaps in a dream or at work.

The ideas will seem unrelated at first, but in time you will have enough elements to begin to see their connection. Then you will understand how your unconscious mind has been tapped to provide creative insights into future potential from the building blocks of past experience. From these insights will come new plans for the future, which you can use to work out present problems.

You may feel that you aren't creative, but everyone is. J. P. Guilford, one of America's pioneers in psychology, did much research to show that creativity is not identical with high intelligence; and psychologist Rollo May showed that the desire for creative expression is a fundamental human need, a need that everyone is capable of fulfilling if he will develop the use of the creative abilities he has.

Notice that the middle segment of the exercise is sleep, which gives the ideas stimulated in the first segment a chance to take form and find a new application to life problems; these new applications may then appear in the third segment following sleep.

You may find it effective to vary the affirmative statements in the autosuggestion step. You can alternate the previously indicated statements with the following affirmations in building self-confidence. They contain a mnemonic device to make remembering them easy. You will notice the underlined letters spell out self-confidence:

1. I am gaining in **S**elf-confidence.
2. I will build an **E**xcellent future.
3. My determination will **L**ast.
4. My **F**irst step is self-acceptance.
5. **Co**nstantly I will grow in this, and **F**irmly **I D**o Exude **N**ew **C**onfidence **E**very day.
6. I am using the **P**ower within to solve problems without.
7. I do this through **F**reedom to choose these attitudes toward life.

If you don't like these affirmations, you can make up a set of your own. The important thing is to say them regularly.

As you practice this basic routine over a period of time, you will become aware of gaining its cumulative benefits. You will see that you can control and use at will the Power within to solve problems. You will know that you are a free person, not a rat in one of Skinner's conditioned response boxes. You will learn how to use this Power to achieve the good things of life, to "find your own bag," to "do you own thing"—in short, to gain a new meaning and purpose in life that will mark you as Somebody. And everybody wants to be Somebody. When you know you are, you will feel the self-confidence needed to tackle Step 4, **Getting Into the Mind-Set Necessary for Discovery of New Meaning and Purpose.**

Chapter VI Step 4

Exercise 1 Expanding Perceptual Awareness
And
Exercise 2 Stimulating Creative Imagination

(These are the types of exercises necessary
to train ourselves in the search for
new meaning in old experience.)

Getting Into the Mind-Set Necessary for Discovery of New Meaning and Purpose

IN ORDER TO progress in discovery of new and more dynamic meaning in life, and to grasp new purposive goals to satisfy our deepest meaning we need to develop new techniques of attack or procedures in ferreting out the goals to fulfill this meaning. There are two basic special techniques which, when practiced consistently, will enable us to do this. They are designed to bring out the creative abilities that we all have in much greater degree than we usually realize, but which we don't learn to use. These techniques are as follows:

1. Expanding conscious awareness, and
2. Stimulating creative imagination.

Let us consider each of these and how it works. First, *expanding conscious awareness*: This means that we must become more aware of the world about us and what goes on in it. For example, if I ask you to look out of the window and tell me what you see, you may reply, "It is a sunny day, and a car is passing by, and there are two children playing in the yard." But if I ask you to take a second look and tell me what else you see, and if I add to your motivation by offering you a reward for each additional thing you can report, you will undoubtedly notice much more than you did the first time.

That is the way it is with our problems. If someone asks us what is wrong, we give a short answer and think that we have said all there is to be said. We don't like to talk about it in the first place, so we say a few words and try to leave it at that. But only by digging into the minute details—by expanding our conscious awareness of the vital and significant implications of the problem—can we hope to work out a new solution to it.

The truth is that this is exactly what many young people are talking about and trying to do when they blow their minds with various harmful drugs. They want to expand their conscious awareness and to see more of life than they have ever been able to see before. And their aim is a good one; the error is in their methodology. Their techniques lead to disastrous side effects and after effects. And in the long run the drugs don't accomplish their goals: They only give a false feeling that you have had some great insights into some new aspect of life; but when the drug effects wear off, these insights are gone.

There is, however, a safe and effective way to expand conscious awareness which we will consider presently.

Second, *stimulating creative imagination*: This is the process of using the creative capacity we all have in potential form. After we have expanded our conscious awareness to become more perceptive of what goes on around us, we need to use these new perceptions creatively. This means that we must put all of our experiences together in new ways, in order to find new meanings in the total pattern of life. When we have analyzed our problems in greater detail and have become aware of all of the aspects we may have previously overlooked, we then must relate all that we have found to the totality of our life experience. This will suggest something new about where we should go from there.

In other words, we use our creative capacities to imagine new solutions to old problems. We do this through relating the new aspects of these problems (of which we have now become aware) to other areas of life (of which we have now also become newly conscious). Such a process puts our problem in a new light and gives us new hope for the future.

And then, without realizing just how it happened, we find ourselves in possession of a new lease on life, a new meaning and purpose, in place of the old feelings of hopelessness and despair: We have achieved the goal of logoanalysis.

The exercises given in this book for both of our two basic techniques will guide you in applying logoanalysis to your particular problems. But first let's turn to an analogy that will illustrate how it all works.

Imagine that your entire life is represented by a large picture. Further suppose that this picture is cut up into a thousand small pieces like a jigsaw puzzle. You have been trying to put the picture together and have succeeded in properly placing most of them, but there are a number of missing segments.

These pieces represent missing elements of your life. That is, they are the failures, conflicts, and troubles with which you are now faced.

In some cases you may be able, at a later date, to find at least a portion of the missing segments. But right now, you don't know where they are, and you see no hope of locating them. In other words, as you view your present troubles, they seem to leave gaps or holes in your life, and you are unable to conceive of any way of filling them.

What if you are never able to find the missing pieces? You may be tempted to draw the conclusion that your life is hopeless and meaningless and that you have nothing left to live for. When you are faced with a severe problem, you will be concentrating on it so completely that you will ignore all of the other aspects of life, even though you may have some very good things going for you.

Thus, you will forget about all of the hundreds of pieces of your life that do fit together and give a real meaning and purpose to the overall picture. You will find it difficult to see the overall picture, although you may be looking right at it, because you are wrapped up in the little segment that represents some current problem.

When the problem is severe, you don't think about anything else at the time. This is very similar to what you would experience in looking at the picture through a long cardboard tube. Suppose you are looking through such a tube at the part of the picture that is circled and that represents your most severe problem. The tube is like the emotional upset that keeps your attention focused on this area of trouble.

Since you can't see anything else except your current trouble, you get the feeling that this is all there is to your life. If this were really true, it would be logical for you to give up in despair, for there would be too many missing pieces to allow you to find much meaning in the few remaining segments in this area. As long as you are looking through the cardboard tube at this one area of your life, as it were, there doesn't seem to be much hope for you.

Seeing the Whole Picture

But suppose someone comes along and knocks the tube out of your hand. Suddenly you see the whole picture of your life at once. Obviously you now see new elements of experience that remind you of important things to live for in spite of your difficulties. You sense a new meaning and purpose in your life as a whole. By comparison, the missing pieces within the circle— which had loomed so large when you were focusing only on this area—now take on far less significance. You wonder how you could have become so wrapped up in this little area of your life that you ignored all of the successes, the hopes and ambitions, and the assets in the rest of it.

Unfortunately, in reality no one can knock this tube out of your hand so that you can see the whole of life at one glance. At the moment, you are forced by circumstances to peer in despair only at the few pieces that can be seen through the tube. How, then, can you work out of this apparently hopeless situation? There is only one way.

That way is to move the tube slowly around, gradually scanning the total picture segment by segment, so that finally you can put all of the parts together and perceive the meaning of the whole. It is a slow process, and you may become discouraged if you do not always remember the final goal. Some of the segments you will look at will have little meaning within themselves, but it is only by relating each segment to every other one that the overall significance of the total picture can at last be perceived.

In other words, when you look at the little slice of life represented by your immediate problem, it seems overpowering and meaningless until you move by association to another area of your past experience, and to another, and to still another. In the long run you will see your successes, your strong points, and your assets—all of which give a new meaning to the whole, a new hope for the future, and minimize the present failures. When you begin to gain a new perspective on the total pattern of your life, you will begin to grasp a total meaning and purpose in life. Thus, you can use the present difficulty as a stepping stone toward a new tomorrow.

A failure can be turned into an asset in the long run when it is seen as a learning experience that helps you attain a future goal—a goal you may not have been prepared to achieve without the prior failure. In this sense, misfortunes can turn out to be blessings in disguise. But to make use of them, you have to explore their relationship to all of the other experiences you have had, and only then will you see what they are supposed to teach you in relationship to your future goals.

This process of "moving the tube around" over the whole picture of life illustrates the two basic techniques of logoanalysis. That is, moving the tube is a matter of *expanding your conscious awareness* of all that has occurred in your past experience and of *stimulating your creative imagination* to put together these segments of past experience in a new and meaningful way. Using these techniques will suggest an ultimate direction or goal that can be achieved.

The exercises are designed to help you explore your life experiences in relation to your present situation. Using them will enable you to find the meaning of the total picture of your life. When you have found it, you will be able to go on from there, in spite of whatever handicaps and difficulties you may face, and to live your life in a way that will give you an identity as Somebody.

This does not mean that only those who have serious problems can profit from this. Life may be going well for you, but you may still sense a need to improve, to find a fresh meaning, a higher purpose. If so, these procedures can help you do it. You may be looking down the cardboard tube, as it were, at a merely boring present situation. Exploring this situation in relation to the many other segments of your total life experience can give you a new perspective. You will see that, by following the exercises, you can achieve success.

EXPANDING PERCEPTUAL AWARENESS

HOW MANY SQUARES?

How many squares do you see in this figure? Sixteen? That's what most people say. But what would you say if we told you there were 30 squares? Deleting the language you might use, we'll venture to say you would respond in the negative. But there really are 30. and you can find them if you stop to remember that we didn't say they all had to be the same size.

Normal perception starts with sixteen. As you expand perceptual awareness you can count the full 30. Go next to 2x2 squares. Here you will find a total of 9. Note that the 2x2 square can start anywhere including the center of the figure. Then go on to 3x3 squares, of which there are 4. And then remember that the figure as a whole is square. Add them up and you'll find 30.

Now you're in the mind frame needed to perceive more in your environment than you had ever noticed before. This is expanding perceptual awareness.

EXPANDING PERCEPTUAL AWARENESS OF MEANINGFUL LIFE EXPERIENCES

Directions: For the past part of your life, recollect all of the very important events that you can:

Date	Negative Event	Date	Positive Event
1.		1.	
2.		2.	
3.		3.	
4.		4.	
5.		5.	
6.		6.	

7.   7.
_____

Of all of these events, which ones meant the most to you?

_____

How do these events influence your life today?

_____

How can you **use** these events to add meaning and purpose to your life in the **future**?

_____

_____

EXERCISE IN EXPANDING AWARENESS OF EVERYDAY EXPERIENCES

From a magazine select a picture you like. Then write:

1. Ten things which you see in the picture.

2. Ten *new* things which you can **imagine** that were not actually in the picture.

3. Why did this picture attract you?

4. Write down **all** of the things which you actually can see in the picture.

5. Now write down all of the additional things which you can *imagine* as you look at details of the picture.

6. The repeated practice of this exercise from time to time will give you an expanded awareness of how much we all miss in everyday life—we miss much of what is going on all around us. But we can reduce this greatly by the simple act of conscious attention to details.

EXERCISES IN CREATIVE IMAGINATION

Write a paragraph on each of the following items:

1. Why do you think human life exists?

2. What do you think is the meaning of your own life? That is, why have all of your particular unique problems happened to you?

3. What will you have to do to fulfill the meaning of your own life? That is, what do your special experiences and unique problems suggest as a life goal or future plan which—if achieved—will give your life meaning and value?

4. What can you do to get started?

5. If you had only one more day to live, how would you spend it? Would this day have any meaning and purpose? If so, what? Write out the answers below:

6. What would you do **today** if you had only one more day to live? Write out below what you did:

"If I owned the world . . . ."

7. If you owned the world, what would you change about it? Name below—in the order of their importance to you—five things which you would most **like** to change:

1. _____

2. _____

3. _____

4. _____

5. _____

8. 1. Name one of the things above which you can really help to change.

    _____

    2. Describe how you plan to work toward this change in the future:

Chapter VII

Step 5

Encounter

Exercise 1

WHERE ARE YOU NOW? AND WHERE ARE YOU GOING?

A. 1. Who loves you? _____

   2. Who cares what happens to you? _____

   3. Who depends upon you? _____

   4. Who respects you? _____

   5. Who looks up to you? _____

B. Who do you wish did each of these?

   1. Love _____

2. Care _____

3. Depends upon _____

4. Respects _____

5. Looks up to _____

C. What can you do to gain these responses from each of these people?

1. Love _____

2. Care _____

3. Dependency upon _____

4. Respect _____

5. Looking up to _____

D. Where you lack any answers to "C" put this aside and think about it later.

Chapter VII

Step 5

Encounter

Exercise 2

THE "EASY ON" EXERCISE: GETTING STARTED

Instructions: In order to learn just how easy it really is to execute the exercises, let's do one that you can do even with your dog:

Mission: To show a positive **attitude** of friendliness, acceptance and approval in respect to **something** about **some** fellow living things. They can be a person or a lower animal or even a plant. Let's start with the easiest one first (the plant)—after **selecting** all three in advance:

Procedure:

1. **Choose:** (1) A plant (tree, flower, weed); (2) a lower animal (dog, cat, bird, horse, kangaroo, and so forth);

(3) a human being—any person with whom you have contact.

2. **Action:** Complete the following *task* for each of the three levels: (1) Use your imagination to react to (per chance to talk to) the plant in an approving way. (2) Do the same to the lower animal you have chosen. (3) Do the same to the person you have chosen. In the latter case you **don't** have to explain that this is part of a planned exercise; just think of something approving, and compliment this person along these lines. (Maybe you like the hair or the suit or the profile or the voice or the way he/she does something.)

3. Be prepared for possible rejection. "You can't win 'em all" especially the first time. (Well, maybe you will win them all, but don't count on it. Actually there is a high probability that you won't fail on this first exercise, but you've got to be prepared because we all fail at times and have to be ready to handle it). if you do fail, mark the score below by circling the minus sign opposite the task you failed; if you succeed, circle the plus sign. You get three times the credit for the person as for the plant. Perfect score on this exercise = 6.

4. **Results:** Complete the form below:

TASK	WHAT YOU ACTUALLY DID	RESPONSE YOU GOT
PLANT		
LOWER ANIMAL		
PERSON		

Chapter VII

Step 5

Encounter

Exercise 3

Developing Relationships That Lead to Encounter

(A) ONE GOOD DEED A DAY KEEPS LONELINESS AWAY

Mission: To do something today that shows some being that you feel kindly toward him/her/it.

Procedure:

1. **Tasks:** Start with a lower animal. **Choose:** (1) A rabbit, dog, cat, squirrel, bird, fish, guinea pig, regular pig, chicken, etc. (2) A human being known to you. (3) A human stranger.
2. **Action:** (1) With the lower animal chosen: (a) Feed it something you know it likes. (b) Pet the animal, first

making sure that it has become friendly toward you. In the case of unpredictable animals, be sure to wear heavy protective gloves. (2) With the human being chosen: Do some kind of favor or helpful action: Carry something for an elderly person.... Ask a question which shows you respect his/ her opinion.... Pay him/ her a compliment.... etc. Start with a family member or friend. (3) With the stranger: Do something helpful: Give directions; wait in your car for him/her to pass first; as a pedestrian wait for him/her to pass first; open a door.... Whatever you can think of that shows courtesy to the stranger.

3. **Results:**

TASK	WHAT YOU ACTUALLY DID	RESPONSE YOU GOT
LOWER ANIMAL		
HUMAN BEING FAMILIAR FRIEND		
HUMAN STRANGER		

Chapter VII

Step 5

Encounter

Exercise 4

Developing Relationships That Lead to Encounter

(B) A DAILY DOSE OF POSITIVE ACTION

Theme: The key to Logotherapy is doing daily exercises in positive action to express good will, kindness, optimism, helpfulness, all of which are behaviors oriented toward love. While we all have to reject behavior which violates our rights, we can still feel altruistic toward the world, and even toward the individual whom we perceive as the cause of our trouble.

1. **Mission:** To practice positive behavior oriented in the direction of love as opposed to hate; to build firm habits of this type of behavior in a program to

reach the stage of altruism in as much daily behavior as possible.

2. **Procedure:**

   1. **Task:** Each morning for one week plan some activity for the day which will **relate** you to someone else in a positive, congenial, happy way and avoid negative confrontations and hostile conflicts in a way that should elicit positive responses and signs of approval from this someone.

   2. **Action:** After planning whatever you will do today, put the plan into action. This is simple enough because you work at your own pace and will make it a part of your daily routine.

Chapter VIII

Step 6

Dereflection

NANCY GOODMAN CAME for counseling because she was suffering from what Frankl calls the human condition of our times, existential vacuum. In spite of a full life for her thirty-five years, she was bored by the failure of a long struggle to find a meaning and purpose that would mark her as Somebody and give her existence a personal identity.

Nan had read *The Doctor and the Soul*, the first of Frankl's books to appear in English, and she was deeply impressed by logotherapy. She was ripe for this approach to human existence, but she was green in applying it. Although she was not sick, she needed help. While she possessed the fullness of material success, she felt empty in spirit. And in spite of the ability to function well in the externals of daily routine, she was inwardly a hollow shell.

I noticed that she was very beautiful and poised the first time she came to see me. "How may I help you, Mrs. Goodman?" I asked as I glanced over the sheet of preliminary data completed by the receptionist.

"I'm hoping you can tell me, Doctor," she answered in a soothing, sultry voice. "I can't really say there is anything wrong. I have a rather full life with no special worries. I ought to be happy, but I'm not. I get so bored sometimes I wish I could take off for the moon. I feel like running from life, but there's no place to go."

I looked again at her data sheet. "You certainly seem to have attained a great deal of success as far as the usual values sought by most people are concerned."

"You mean that I've enough money for comfort, that I've had a successful business career, and that I've had the time to devote to my special interests. And, I suppose, that I've always been reasonably successful in whatever I've undertaken."

"Well, largely, yes. But you have failed in one area—marriage. You've had two unsuccessful marriages."

Nancy glared at me. "Oh, that. You seem to be assuming, Doctor, that we women live only for the glory of being accepted by men. Well, I've got news for you, Doctor. We females can make it just fine without men, and doing so is not a mark of failure."

"Agreed. But in that case, why did you want to marry in the first place?"

She resisted entrapment. "The first time I was young and didn't know any better, and I wanted to get out of the straight jacket in which my stuffy parents kept me. And the second time I found a man—the president of a large department store where I was the head buyer—who could have been a worthy husband. But he wasn't interested in sharing my life or in helping me develop my true potential. He was concerned mostly with his own achievements. He considered me only an expensive decoration, a luxury to take off the shelf and play with when the mood hit. I didn't feel at all bad about taking him in the divorce for enough to make myself comfortable. He had a good lesson coming."

"You sound rather vindictive. And this means you feel you

are the one who failed, and that the other person came out ahead."

Nancy didn't like that remark at all. "No, I'm not vindictive. I really feel sorry for him. He doesn't know how to live; all he knows is work. In spite of his success, he has never found himself."

"But isn't this just what you said about yourself? In spite of your success, you haven't found what you want in life, have you?"

Nancy was silent, but it was the kind of silence that gives consent. I started again to review her case history.

The story of her past life was varied and exciting. She was the only child of middle-class Protestant parents. Her father was an accountant; her mother, a housewife. The family had been strictly establishment, a dutiful cog in the post-World War II "organization man" machine. For them the life goal was suburban security, with two cars under the carport and a boat on the lake; and the way to get these blessings was to line up with the status quo and its power structure.

For Nancy this was not only a life of boredom and meaninglessness, but also a hypocritical surface endorsement of traditional values that served only those in power. And she felt that such values were held in secret contempt and flagrantly violated by these same men and women. In high school Nancy began to disdain this hypocrisy; in college she broke into open rebellion; and in the business world she actively sabotaged the system.

As a college freshman and sorority pledge with bids from several sororities, she was popular with the fraternity boys. One of the males took advantage of her distress over a quarrel with the housemother and persuaded her to elope and marry. But within a few months she was disillusioned. He proved to be a rascal who wanted her to go to work and support him while he went to school. She went to the divorce court instead and then back to her family.

Returning to college, she majored in business administration, but upon graduation she found only secretarial work, for which she blamed sex prejudice. She had the initiative to find a way out, and within a year she became private secretary to the president of a large department store.

During the next several years she was a popular, but selective, woman courted by—among others—her aging multimillionaire boss. She diplomatically fended off his advances, while leaving him enough hope to keep open the door of any advantageous contacts he could offer.

Through one of these contacts she obtained a position as buyer with his chief competitor, the city's other big department store. Of course, her former boss was furious; in fact, he became so angry that he had a mild paralytic stroke and, as a result, had to relinquish the presidency to his son Kenneth. Unknown to the father and largely in defiance of him, Kenneth had also courted Nancy with the same dubious success.

A year passed, during which his son played a double gambit. Partly to retrieve Nancy from dangerous competition, and partly to prove his manhood to be greater than that of his father, he continued to pursue her. Nancy was no fool; she learned buying quickly and well. Without giving or promising herself, she accepted Kenneth's offer to return to the old company in the capacity of head buyer.

This outraged her former associates, no subordinates, with more experience and expectations of the position for themselves. It also caused her former boss, now retired, to have a second stroke. He died shortly thereafter.

Kenneth was now the chief executive and principal stockholder of the company, and this multiplied correspondingly his stock with Nancy. Within a year they were married, and she retired from an active company role.

Yes, this unscrupulous woman had learned to play well the organization man's game and to beat him at it. She was now the power behind the executive throne, and for a time she found a real personal identity in this role. She prodded her husband to greater and greater success, and when he faltered or stumbled, she put him back on course.

But she had made one fatal mistake: She had taught him too efficiently. For her, competitive success had been only a game at which she must prove herself superior. This was her answer to the galling early rejection of her feminine status. But for Kenneth these goals became ends in themselves, and he soon lost sight of his wife in the struggle.

At first she was so busy enjoying the power of her new position that she did not notice what had happened. As the wife of one of the city's wealthiest and leading citizens, her advice, membership, opinion, and support were sought for many kinds of causes. Civic enterprises and social events, which previously would have been closed to her, now enlisted her in leading capacities.

And if she didn't find activities to her liking, she was in a position to create them. This she did not hesitate to do, even at considerable expense, for she had unlimited charge accounts and credit, and her husband was too absorbed in making money to notice how she was spending it.

So Nancy adopted and soon discarded a rapid succession of causes, ranging from a variety of charities, through free Sunday afternoon symphonies, little theatre, amateur opera, and psychic research.

As a young girl she had tried ballet dancing, acting, painting, writing, and singing. She had a little talent, but not enough to score well in any area. In response to a marginal awareness of this fact, she had been given to moods of depression and withdrawal. But her strong drive to be Somebody had always forced her out of a failed project and into something new.

The more she searched for fulfillment and failed, the more conscious she grew of the emptiness of her marriage, and the more nauseated she became by her husband who epitomized the values she held in contempt. She was resentful of his ignorance of, and unconcern for, her inner feelings of restless boredom—the boredom that signals the presence of Frankl's existential vacuum.

The outcome was hardly surprising. Before Kenneth realized what had happened, his wife and a sizeable chunk of his fortune had passed through the divorce court and out of his life.

Both he and Nancy were satisfied to go their own way. Kenneth was unhappy but did not know it because he was not aware that his life's passion for money and power was an inadequate substitute for a mission he had never found. Nancy was unhappy, but she knew it because she was aware that she needed such a mission, and had not found it. Of the two, Nancy was in the more hopeful position.

Following the divorce Nancy embarked upon a major effort to find herself. During the next two years she tried many things.

At first she thought politics would fill the void. She ran for the city council, and her charm captured votes. But she couldn't keep her mind on the town's business, and was gone on so many trips during meeting times that the council censured her. She seized the chance to resign and to blame antifemale prejudice.

Next, she decided to try religion. A natural reaction to her strict upbringing was to reject the confinement of the Judeo-Christian tradition and to turn to oriental thought. A logical direction was Zen Buddhism.

So Nancy read a lot of Zen and studied with an Indian Guru. But meditation upon a mystical *Koan* (such as, what is the sound of one hand clapping?) did not feed her need for literal soul food. Soon she dropped Zen.

She tried in rapid succession Christian Science (too ethereal), Spiritualism (too mystical), Baha'i (too square—no drinking, and all that), Reform Judaism (too selective—no dilettantes welcome), Catholicism (too establishment), and Unitarianism (too intellectual and emotionally antiseptic).

Maybe the spiritual union she sought could be found only in a more concrete relationship. It occurred to her that this might materialize only in a truly fulfilling sex experience—

perhaps a lover would bring her into harmony with the Eternal. She had had her fill of marriage, and she had never had a genuinely satisfying sex life. That's what was missing, she thought.

About this time, Nancy met Roger, an unconscionable scoundrel who persuaded her to accept him as her sexual partner. The affair lasted only a few months.

"What a slimy s.o.b. he turned out to be!" Nancy recalled. "I trusted him fully, and gave myself completely to him. When he put his arms around me, he was reaching for my checkbook behind my back. That's how he repaid me."

However, Nancy did gain some benefit from the experience. She discovered that sex was not the answer to her problem.

So what was the solution? Nancy was running down in her floundering quest. Finally, it occurred to her that she was running *from* something within herself, rather than *toward* something. Of course, she had marginally known this all along, but would not face it until she was exhausted from the flight.

This was when she came for help. After having read Frankl's book, which fortunately coincided with her exhaustion, she was ripe for the insight into what had been happening and for awareness that she needed guidance in working herself out of the fog.

"Let's see where we go from here," I said after we had discussed her case history. "You're looking for the right thing— a place to put your life that will pull the pieces together and give it a new meaning and purpose. But so far you've looked in all of the wrong places. What is left? Where else is there to look, that you have not yet explored?"

"I'm about out of ideas," she confessed, "but I have considered some other possibilities. For example, I might go back to school, and take all kinds of courses, until I find my thing."

"That's a partially good idea," I agreed. "It won't do the job alone, but you could undoubtedly profit—like most people— from a broader basic education. This is a fundamental source of ideas. You could attend adult education classes at night and on weekends, if you want to, so that you would have plenty of time for any special area of interest that develops."

"Yes, there are so many problems in the world today that anyone can find something that is special to him. But my problem seems to be that nothing lasts. I've been seriously interested in everything I've tried, and at first all of them seemed to be it. Then after awhile they would all fade, and I'd begin to be bored again, and disillusioned and restless, and I'd have to start over."

"Why do you think this happens? Why can't you maintain an interest?"

"I wish I knew, Doctor. That's why I'm here. Why doesn't anything last? What's the matter with me? Or is the world crazy?"

"The world's crazy, but that's not why you can't find yourself. Your basic problem is that you've tried to solve it by taking vacations."

"What?"

"I mean that you've tried to solve conflicts by running from them, just as if you took a vacation and expected the trouble to go away by the time you returned. Each of your safaris into the unknown in search of a purpose has really been an escape from facing what is missing in your life, rather than—as it seemed on the surface—a direct attack upon the problem."

"You mean that my real life purpose involved some obstacle I don't want to face? Yes, I've thought that at times, but I don't know what it is."

"I think it's an obstacle of which you're not aware."

"Well, what is it, for God's sake?"

"I don't know."

"You don't know! That's a big help. Thanks for nothing!"

"Simmer down, Nancy. I don't know—yet. And you don't know. But together we will find out."

"All right, Doctor. I don't know where you're going, but I'll go along for awhile."

"Good. Now I want to tell you the story of someone else who faced pretty much the same search for meaning in life with which you are struggling, and who experienced about the same frustration. As a matter of fact, a lot of people could give you a parallel picture."

"Really? I sort of thought—"

"You thought, as most of us do, that nobody else has problems just like yours."

"Yes, I guess—"

"Your experience is basically what Frankl calls the 'collective neurosis of our times'—the existential vacuum left by a lack of a sense of meaning and purpose in life, due largely to the human condition today. It's something we all have to face and overcome in this computerized machine age. And we each run into our own special hang-ups in conquering it. There is no standard formula to deal with it; we have to tailor the answer to our own individual life experiences. And yours—like those of many other people—involve some special hang-up that has to be worked out before you can find your purpose. It is this hang-up that we have to uncover together."

"That sounds okay. But how?"

"I think you'll understand the problem better after I tell you this story, which will illustrate how human this struggle is, and how similar your feelings are to those of others who have faced it."

"Is this your own life story, Doctor?"

"No. Mine you'd never believe anyway. Do you know anything about Mount Kilimanjaro?"

"I think—it's a mountain in Africa, isn't it? Didn't Hemingway write something about it?"

"Yes. It is the tallest peak on the African continent. Rising about twenty thousand feet above sea level, it is perennially snowcapped. Animals seldom venture above the timber line, for there's no food or shelter and nothing they'd want. But in the twenties a party of explorers who succeeded in scaling the western summit found near the top the dried and frozen carcass of a leopard. No one has ever explained what the leopard sought at this altitude. But from this simple story, which appeared in the public press, Ernest Hemingway spun one of his greatest stories."

"Oh—yes, I think I remember a movie, something about the snow on that mountain."

"That's right. It was from Hemingway's short story, *The Snows of Kilimanjaro*. The story is only about nine thousand words long, but it contains in a nutshell the whole picture of man's search for meaning in life."

"I remember that the snowcapped peak was supposed to be some kind of a symbol of life to the hero."

"The hero was a writer, Harry, who had been unable to write for awhile. He seemed to have lost his creativity. In an effort to find inspiration, he returned on a safari with is latest mistress to an accessible level on Mount Kilimanjaro, because he had once been there during his most productive period. The mountain had become a mystical symbol of the elusive quality of meaning in life, the meaning Harry had struggled without success to find. He thought that once he was back on the mountain, things would begin to fall into place. But he contracted blood poisoning, transportation broke down, and his lover attempted to care for him while they sent for help. The help did not arrive in time, however, and he died. His last thoughts were a fantasy that a plane came to take him to the hospital. But after the aircraft took off with him, it suddenly changed course and headed directly into the snowcapped summit. As it was about to hit, Harry experienced a revelation that the peak contained the ultimate meaning of life, which he was at last going to understand."

Nancy was uncomfortable. "You are saying that I, like Harry, have been trying to find my way to the mountain top. Are you also saying that, like him, I'll find what I'm seeking only in death?"

"Not necessarily, although that's true of a lot of Harrys—and there are millions of him. In fact, Hemingway himself was probably the model for his character, for he struggled all of his life to attain this same knowledge of the ultimate values in human existence. He found what he considered at least partial answers that fit his own experience and gave it meaning, but the meaning was illusory and capricious—he could not maintain it consistently. At times he felt that all of his work was worthless, and that nothing was lasting. In a fit of such despair he committed suicide."

"You think I might do that?"

"You have not shown this trend of personality so far. But you no doubt feel like checking out at times, just as most of us do. It all depends upon how you handle things from now on. You came for help because you are close to the end of your rope in the search for your own meaning. As we've said, your trouble lies in the fact that some hang-up, at present unknown, has kept you from finding a stable and permanent meaning for your own life. Now we must explore together in a systematic way all of the areas of human value in an effort to find, first, what you want that would give life meaning, and second what hang-up blocks this attainment. When we find where the problem is, we can work it out. Then you can settle upon a life goal that should be satisfying on a permanent basis."

"What do you mean—explore in a systematic way all human values?"

"That's what we are coming to. I am going to give you a series of exercises as homework assignments."

"You mean it's going to be like going back to school?"

"These exercises are quite grown-up. There is no mental strain—although you may sweat emotionally at times, because they will lead you to face yourself and your real, deepest inner feelings, and this often isn't pleasant. This type of homework isn't the school kind—although, as you yourself suggested school might not be a bad idea for you. While we are working, why don't you take a couple of courses in the university extension department? It might be best not to take the courses for credit. Since you already have a degree, the university will let you audit courses. Take courses in such things as literature, science, history, sociology, and the like, because they will help you get a broad picture of the whole panorama of human experience, and that is what you need."

"Yes, but don't you think I should also take some psychology and philosophy?"

"No—unless perhaps you can find a survey course in philosophical thought. I don't think you'll get what you need in technical courses in either of these fields. The truth is that most of the psychology and philosophy that really helps one to understand man is not found in the textbooks, but in literature. Shakespeare knew more of both fields than all of the professors alive today."

Nancy laughed. "You're probably right. Yes, I like to read, and I like literature and history. I think trying some courses would be fun."

"The idea is to expose yourself to as broad a variety of human experience as possible," I continued. "Only in this way will you find what is there for you. You've already had experiences with a number of different aspects of life, but you have not found your own identity. The next step is to look through the eyes of others, vicariously sharing their experiences in order to absorb whatever may be meaningful to you. Reading and listening to what people have to say will help. And the exercises I give you will stimulate your thinking, as you work to integrate all of these life experiences with your own. This is a process of analyzing the elements that offer something to you, and of synthesizing these into a sense of meaning and purpose that will make your life worthwhile."

So we began the exercises. At first Nancy thought some of them made little sense; others were fun; and to still others, she was indifferent. This is the way with most who try them. You can't see where they are leading until you get fairly far along.

These exercises are not cure alls. I would not deceive anyone into believing they are—and they were not for Nancy. There is no simple, easy road to finding a personal identity, but this identity exists for all who are willing to pay the price of persistence in the search.

A few months passed before Nancy began to see where her real hang-up had been, the blocking factor that had kept her from finding permanent satisfaction in any life goal. I could, of course, see it much sooner, but I knew she must discover it for herself.

The answer was elementary: In spite of her lifelong reaction against the establishment, her deepest feelings were quite conventional. And this is true of most who overreact against tradition. She really wanted a stable marriage, children, and a vine-covered cottage. She also needed the additional creative outlet of a cause in whose behalf she could find a unique identity apart from her family.

Many women today feel this double need for the feminine role and the crusader's role. Successful family men have always had dual identities. In the past women identified with their husbands to the extent of sharing vicariously both roles, but in today's age of individuality this identification has grown far less effective.

Nancy did develop plans for the accomplishment of both roles, and she did lose her emotionally charged negativism toward traditional society. She did not lose—or need to—the reaction against hypocritical lip service to traditional values.

She met a physician from another state who worked with the underprivileged. This friendship forged her interest in becoming a graduate social worker. She left the city to begin working toward her graduate degree, and I lost track of her. I can't be certain that she found her purpose in life, but her previous progress suggests that she did.

Now it is time for you to find your purpose in life. This brings us to the exercise designed to aid in exploring your assets in spite of all handicaps.

Chapter VIII

Step 6

Exercise

USING THE ASSETS YOU HAVE
IN SPITE OF ALL POSSIBLE HANDICAPS

"DEREFLECTION"

Part A

List all of the **liabilities** of which you can think:

Part B

List all of the **assets** of which you can think:

Part C

1. What especially meaningful experiences can you remember over your entire life?

2. What *value* (in your personal system of values) made each experience meaningful?

3. From what future experiences could you probably derive similar satisfactions to parallel each of these past experiences?

4. What dreams of flash visions do you have?

5. What realistic methods can you think of to achieve each of these dreams?

6. What are your present greatest strengths in life?

7. What immediate plans do you now have upon completing this present program?

8. What are your long-range plans for the future?

9. What realistic hope do you see for the future? (Before you say none or not much, consider some of the strengths which you have already noted in the second part of this exercise).

Exercise 1 The Final Scene: Commitment Analysis of the New Life Goals to Which You Will Be Committed Directions: Indicate below the areas of life in which you have now found personal **meaning**. Write out fully the specific goals which have become meaningful to you in each area. In each instance the goals must be regarded by you as important to your future and as reasonably possible of attainment. Areas of **activity:** Specific life goals which challenge you to achievement. These areas represent the way in which you will occupy your time.

A1. Vocation(s) _____

A2. Avocation(s) (hobbies) _____

A3. Causes for which to work (political, religious, social, civic: clubs, schools, organizations, groups of all types)

Areas of **value:** The areas of personal meaning which underlie your activities. Meanings are always found in **encounter** relationships beyond the individual. Meanings are personal, while values are cultural. But all possible cultural areas of value must be explored in order to find the ones which give your own life personal meaning.

B1. Home and family _____

B1-1. Spouse _____

B1-2. Children _____

B1-3. Relations _____

B1-4. Pets _____

B2. Other interpersonal relationships. _____

_____

B2-1. Friends _____

B2-2. Work associates _____

B2-3. Others _____

B3. "Spiritual" encounter. _____

B3-1. Encounter with nature _____

B3-2. Encounter with Higher Power _____

_____

Do you want something listed here enough to sacrifice whatever you have to in order to gain it? Enough to sweat out the pressures of life without copping out through alcohol or other means of escape from facing these pressures? Until you can say yes to these questions, you have not found a real meaning in life.

Chapter IX

Step 7-2-1

Exercise 2 Analysis of Your New Life Goals Self-Revaluation and Commitment.

THE CRUX OF this step is to analyze the life goals that you have developed. From them you should have formed a picture of the values that are most meaningful to you, and of practical plans of action through which you will be able to actualize these meanings. In fact, you should have already begun to implement these plans and to experience the satisfaction of progress.

That leads to the crucial final phase, *commitment:* The key to establishing a valid meaning and purpose to give you a personal identity and the experience of being Somebody lies in wholehearted devotion to, and faith in, some life goals. Here you may well encounter some of the doubts and frustrations that beset Ralph. Here you must face and conquer them as he finally did.

Sources of Help

In this final step there are some sources of help:

Discussion and interpersonal interaction. It helps—just as it did with Ralph—to talk about your feelings, fears, and doubts as you contemplate the problem of a life goal. There are several possibilities for a suitable person to listen to you:

A *therapist or counselor*. This is usually the best overall choice if it is available. Do not forget the admonition given in Chapter 1 to evaluate very carefully whether you have any symptoms, and if so, to obtain a medical check-up and opinion of your need for professional help. If you are not in need of psychiatric help, the best source of counseling may be a priest, minister, or rabbi. Exercise precautions in selection. A clergyman who is self-righteous, vindictive, narrow-minded or overly critical can destroy you. On the other hand, an understanding, sympathetic, progressive and well-trained clergyman is often your best source of help. In fact, such a man will frequently have training in pastoral counseling, which qualifies him as a member of a mental health team. If you can find one with this training, he is likely to give you more valuable assistance in the search for, and commitment to, a life meaning than you can get anywhere else. Remember that the sincere clergyman will not expect you to become religious, if you are not already, in order to receive his help.

A *friend*. A wise friend can be a sounding board who can help you to understand your hidden motives. An unwise friend can be worse than an enemy. So consider carefully how understanding a person is before making a choice.

A *teacher* (if you are a student). The same precautions in selection apply here as to a friend.

Reading. While you are marking time in making final decisions as to life goals and how much of life you are willing to commit to them, it is a good idea to get away from this book for awhile and to read in related inspirational areas. By all means you should read the basic works of the late Viktor Frankl, M.D., Ph.D., logotherapy's founder, and of some of the other writers in this field. You will also get inspiration from many other books. Go to a good public library and look over the listings in practical psychology and personality development. The works of Dale Carnegie, Mother Teresa, Maxwell Maltz, Norman Vincent Peale, Fulton J. Sheen, Joshua L. Liebman, "Dr. Phil" McGraw, Pope John Paul II, Peter Drucker, Maya Angelo, and others may help you to make a final choice.

Meditation or encounter. Chapter VII Step 5 can help you not only in this final stage of commitment to a life goal, but also in the long-range maintenance of this commitment. Once well established, this procedure makes an excellent lifelong habit that can give strength and direction in times of trouble and frustration, even after you have chosen and have progressed far toward the realization of your commitment.

I can truthfully tell you that, in my own case, meditation has helped me more than any other method of logoanalysis. I have conducted my own version of it every morning and again every evening continuously for a decade. I have missed only one session in all of this time. I stuck to it through two hurricanes, an overnight demonstration stay in a civil defense fallout shelter, and several days' hospitalization, for a minor operation. It takes about a year for meditation to become an established part of your life; after that, it blends as a feature of your personality.

A logoanalytic encounter group. This is basically the procedure which Ralph, whose case was described in this chapter, used in coming to grips with his difficulty in commitment. It worked for him, and it can do the same for you. Please notice that this kind of mutual study group is not the type of activity commonly referred to as an encounter group. The methods are quite different. Here are some rules to follow in conducting a logoanalytic encounter:

(1) Select several friends who are interested in finding a meaning and purpose in their lives. Have at least three

but no more than ten (preferably five to eight) in the group. As interest grows, the group should be split into two groups in order to limit the size of each to the number that can efficiently interact.

(2) Take turns in having the group meet weekly at each home for an hour or two.

(3) The session should be informal, with no officers, dues or other means whereby a manipulating leader might see an opportunity to gain control to feed his own ego. Here a lesson from the experience of Alcoholics Anonymous is in order. The founders of this movement have pointed to the wisdom of such policies in order to prevent misuse of the group. Let the leader for each session be the one who hosts it for that meeting.

(4) Each member should have access to this book and be interested in working through all of the exercises. The function of the group is to offer mutual discussion, suggestions, and encouragement to each individual member in completing his exercises. As a member finishes, sets life goals, and demonstrates commitment to them, his is in a "graduate" position to be of maximum help to the other members.

(5) If several groups are formed in the community, a joint meeting every couple of months (which will probably require obtaining club quarters for the occasion) will be mutually beneficial. At these meetings, the program should center on a talk by some member on some aspect of the problems which he has experienced in completing one of the steps of logoanalysis, and the solutions which he has found. Groups should take turns in furnishing a speaker for these joint sessions.

In concluding this **final step**, look back over your life. Can you see an overall pattern of meaning in all of the things that have happened? Can you spot a destiny or fate, a purpose, a meaning in terms of some job you have been given to do in life? What do all of these experiences lead toward or focus upon in the way of a *raison d'etre* or reason for being?

From your life experiences, as you become aware of them through the exercises of logoanalysis, will come an answer. Do not expect it easily or quickly. The point is illustrated by the title of Somerset Maugham's novel, *The Razor's Edge*, and by this same struggle from the sacred literature of India:

> The sharp edge of a razor is difficult
> to pass over: Thus say the wise the
> path of salvation is hard.
>
> Katha-Upanishad

INDEX

Abigail Van Buren 41
abstract 63, 64, 89
Act as If 105, 107-111
Adler, Alfred 20
agape 32-34, 157
agoraphobia 45
Alcoholics anonymous 72, 103, 149, 172, 191, 238
alienation 12, 120, 148
anxiety 44, 76, 100, 176
apologia pro vita *sua* 13, 35
Armstrong, Kitty 118
artificial relationships 153
attitudes 21, 35, 42, 51, 62, 68, 109, 168, 193
attitudinal value 43, 73, 172

Bacon, Francis 98
Baha'i 136, 222
Beethoven, Ludwig van 61
behavior 19, 22, 29, 30, 31, 33-35, 37, 43, 44, 49, 50, 52, 53, 62, 70, 81, 107, 180, 190, 215, 216
blackmail 122
body language 30
boredom 37, 133, 136, 219, 222
boring 62, 117, 199

Boudreaux, Martial 88, 187
Brande, Dorothea 103

capable 89, 187, 192
Captain Newman, M.D. 35, 36
cardboard tube 115, 117, 197, 199
Cases 33, 41, 45, 58, 77, 94, 110, 114, 120, 125, 129, 176, 196
Catholicism 136, 222
caveat 32, 41, 56, 58, 60, 95, 97
Cerman, Eugene A. 78
Christian Science 136, 222
"Christophied" 32
Churchill, Winston 77, 177
claustrophobia 45
collective neurosis 139, 225
commitment 22, 28, 33, 34, 51, 59, 87, 94, 108, 145, 146, 148, 152, 156, 157, 233, 235-238
common goals 153
common interests 148, 154
companionship 118
compensation 46
conflict 40, 41, 43, 46, 62, 63, 71, 93, 128, 171
conscious awareness 30, 112, 113, 116, 117, 194, 195, 199
covert 31, 38, 56, 96
creative 27, 94, 112-114, 117, 143, 189, 191, 192, 194-196, 199, 206, 229
creative abilities 112, 192, 194
crusader's role 143, 229

depression 39, 44, 95, 100, 106, 135, 145
dereflection 16, 131, 144, 217, 230
despair 78, 109, 114-116, 152, 156, 157, 178, 196-198
Determination 39, 47, 57, 58, 64
determinism 69, 72, 169, 172
direct attack 46, 138
discouragement 107, 152

discovery 11, 15, 26, 40, 111, 112, 193, 194
disillusioned 128, 134, 138, 219, 224
dog 80, 171, 179, 180, 211
Douglas, Kirk 37
drive 48, 108, 118, 135, 221
drugs 35, 113, 127, 195
Drummond, Henry 98

Easter, Ralph 145
Einstein, Albert 62
Ellis, Albert 73, 163, 173
Emotionally intimate 29
Encounter 117, 118, 209, 211, 213, 215
Encounter Groups 152
Enzo Stuarti 36, 37
equality 50
eros 32
ESP 82, 181
existential vacuum 35, 62, 131, 139
Existentialism 70, 169, 170
existentialist 70, 77, 119, 169, 177
expanding 113, 116, 195
Expanding Perceptual Awareness 15, 27, 113, 199, 200, 202
experience 17, 24-27, 38, 57, 70, 76, 77, 79-82, 85, 86, 88, 89, 92, 94, 100, 101, 109, 110, 111, 113, 115-117, 123, 134, 137, 139, 141, 142, 145, 155, 170, 175, 176, 179, 180, 181, 185-187, 190, 192, 194, 196, 198, 199, 220, 225, 228, 235, 238

failure 28, 38, 40, 42, 43, 46, 73, 94, 109, 116, 129, 131, 132, 143, 146, 147, 151, 154, 171, 173, 198, 217, 218
false personal sacrifice 32
Falwell, Jerry 62, 163
fauna and flora 19
feminine role 143, 229
femininity 51

FIRST ATTENDS THE EFFECT (FATE) 59, 60, 64
flywheel 107
Frankl, Viktor E. 11, 14, 23, 35, 190
free will 70, 189, 191
freedom to choose 128, 193
Freud, Sigmund 14, 19, 43, 51
Fry, Patrica L. 99
fulfillment 54, 66, 120, 126, 135, 221

gender 67
genius 24, 38, 39, 40
George Sanders 35
girl taxi driver 92
Goodman, Nancy 131, 217
Grahm, Billy 74, 163, 173
great depression of the thirties 39
Grey's Elegy 66

Heidegger, Martin 77, 177
Heisenberg Uncertainty Principal 76, 175
Hemingway, Ernest 140, 162, 226
hidden power 48
Higher Power 69, 75, 78, 80, 81, 86-89, 169, 175, 177, 178, 180, 181, 185, 234
hopeless 59, 70, 109, 198
human condition 131, 139, 217, 225
human existence 131, 141, 217, 227
human values 141, 227
Hypochondrias 45

Ideas 21, 22, 27, 29, 137, 138, 146, 150, 151, 154, 192, 223, 224
imagination 104, 212
immediate 26, 40, 43, 54, 64, 116, 232
immortality 71, 171
ineffability 76

instinctive 19, 20, 29, 32
Intentionality 40
Intimacy 14, 17, 18, 20-22, 29, 36, 39, 40, 48, 55, 56, 62, 157, 166
intimate relations 18
intimate relationships 29
intuitive 68, 153

jigsaw 114, 196
Joyce Brothers 41
Judeo-Christian 136, 222

Kelly, Orville 35
King, Alexander 126
King, Martin Luther, Jr. 61, 162
Kinsey 119
Kroc, Ray 25
Kubler—Ross, M.D., Elizabeth 76, 175, 176
Kushner, Rabbi 97

learning 128
Leslie, Robert 76, 176
level of *agape* 32
life 11, 13-16, 19, 22-28, 32-41, 44, 45, 47-49, 51, 53, 55, 58, 60-74, 76-82, 86-88, 90-92, 94-97, 100, 104-106, 112-118, 120, 125-128, 131-133, 136-153, 155-157, 161, 162, 164-173, 175-178, 180-182, 185-190, 193-199, 202-206, 217-219, 222, 224-229, 231-239
life mission 157
life purpose 72, 138, 224
lighting 21, 27, 98
"logic—tight compartments" 43
logoanalysis 14, 114, 116, 145, 156, 168, 182, 196, 199, 237, 239
logos 23

logotherapy 14
love 23, 32-35
Luce, Claire Booth 100

magical power of sex 126
Make Today Count 36
Maltz, Maxwell 103, 237
Man's Search For Meaning 23, 35
marathon 152
Masters and Johnson 119
Mc Donald's 25
Maughan, Somerset 151, 239
meaning 22-25, 27, 28, 32, 36, 37, 55, 60, 67, 69, 112, 114, 141, 152, 157, 165, 166, 168, 169, 172, 173
Meaning of Life 13, 140, 166, 226
meaningful relationship 123
meaningless 70, 77, 78, 85, 114, 116, 179, 176, 177, 178, 185, 197, 198
mechanism 63, 69, 71, 169
mechanistically oriented behavioral scientists 34
mind-set 26, 111, 112
missing pieces 114, 115, 196, 197
mission 47, 72, 127, 136, 146, 149, 157, 171, 211, 213, 215, 222
"Mister-In-Between" 28
mores 49, 50-53
music 32, 36, 61, 62, 83, 86, 182, 186

narcissism 107
New Yorkers 34
nonecclesiastical 97

Obsessive—Compulsive Disorders 45
occupational competition 30
Olson, Richard 75, 175
overpowering 116, 198
overt 31, 38, 56

paraphysiological 118
Parapsychology 81, 82, 84, 85
patterns 22, 42, 45, 49, 50, 85, 154, 185, 192
Peale, Norman V. 102, 163, 237
Persistence 24, 26, 39, 40, 41, 47, 57, 58, 64, 72, 143, 171, 228
Personal Relationship 119, 126, 153
philia 32
philosophy 70, 102, 108, 169
phobias 45
physical intimacy 29
"Press On" plaque 24
PON with PAD (press on now with persistence and determination) 58
positivistic science 69, 169
positive 25, 28, 42, 43, 57, 70, 79, 102, 107, 108, 110, 162, 178, 192, 211, 215, 216
potential for success 150
Power of Freedom Exercise 105, 111, 189, 191
power of personal relationships 126
power of positive action 102, 107
power of positive thinking 102, 108
Presence 86, 87, 186
Press On; PO 24
principles 26
problem 141
Procedure 1 29
Procedure 2 30
Procedure 3 30
Procedure 4 31
professional ethics 122
programmed development 58
psychiatrist 14, 20, 35, 43, 75, 76, 85, 86, 90
psychological 44, 45, 71, 77, 94, 118, 121, 169, 170, 171, 176, 192
"pure chance" 78, 85, 177, 185

purpose of life 35
puzzle *see jigsaw puzzle*

Rabbi 33, 97, 236
rain 17, 22, 25, 27, 28
raison d' etre 13, 23, 239
Rationalization 42, 43
"raw sex" 48
Reductionism 71, 170
reductionsts 34, 69
Reform Judaism 136, 222
relationship 18, 29-31, 33, 55, 94, 116, 118, 119, 123, 128, 137, 153, 198, 199, 222
Religion 49, 61, 88, 128, 149
religious 13, 24, 49, 61, 68, 71, 72, 76, 86-88, 90, 95-97, 119, 170, 172, 173, 175, 186, 188, 190, 191, 233, 236
responsibility 49, 59, 60, 64, 73, 78, 128, 129, 151, 173
revolution 21, 50, 52
Rhine, J.B. 82, 162, 181
roots 17, 19, 20, 35
Rorschach Inkblot Test 85, 185
Rorschach, Hermann 85, 185
routine 31, 127, 132, 154, 216

Sartre, Jean-Paul 70, 73, 88, 169, 170, 173, 187
Scheler, Max 71, 171
science 61, 69, 71, 82, 85, 128, 142, 169, 171, 175, 181, 227
scriptures 49
search for meaning 23, 35, 139, 140, 149, 225, 236
self deception 129
self-confidence 26, 60, 90, 97, 102, 111, 145, 188, 189, 191, 193
self-deprecation 109
self-fulfillment 157, 182
Sept. 11, 2001 34
severe 35, 44, 47, 114, 115

sex 14, 17, 18, 20-23, 29, 35, 41, 47-49, 62, 68, 91, 92, 94, 118, 119, 212, 212, 124, 125, 134, 137, 148, 151, 157, 165, 220, 223
Sex relations 23
sexual 17-20, 22, 27, 30, 32, 35, 50-53, 59, 62, 68, 93, 94, 118, 119, 122, 137, 223
Sexual intercourse 18, 22, 94, 119
sexual overtone 30
sexual satiation effect 92, 93
Shakespeare, William 163
She-ma 98
Significant Others 27, 28, 37, 118
Silverman, Dr. Phillis 100
situations 64, 99, 110, 154, 190
Skinner, B. F. 169
social competition 30
Somebody or SOMEBODY 13, 28
"*sour grapes*" 42
Spencer, Herbert 86, 185
spirit 131, 148, 217
spiritual 27, 24, 68, 71, 95-98, 120, 136, 170, 222, 234
Spiritualism 136
stages of grief 100
Step One 66
Step Two 91
Step Three 102, 189
Step Four 112, 194
Step Five 118, 209, 211, 213, 215
Step Six 131, 217, 230
Step Seven 145, 235
Stimulating Creative Imagination 112, 113, 194, 195
storm 21, 23
sub-cultures 50
sublimation 46
sub-rosa 96

successful 14, 26, 35, 46, 63, 91, 98, 102, 109, 110, 132, 143, 218, 229
successful techniques of adjustment 46
suicide 108, 227
superficial 18
superficial love 126
superhuman 118
supernatural 71, 74, 171, 174
"sweet lemon" 42

technique 40, 41, 47, 108-110
techniques 46, 85, 112-114, 116, 117, 185, 194-196, 199
teleological 73, 74, 86, 87, 171, 174, 185
T-groups 152, 153
The Doctor and the Soul 131, 217
The power of passionate purpose 36
The Razor's Edge 151, 239
The Snows of Kilimanjaro 140, 226
The Unheard Cry for Meaning 77, 176
The University of Texas Tower 36
thunder 23, 25, 27
Tipler, Frank 71
traditional 49, 51, 90, 133, 143, 219, 229

ultimate goal of all true love 34
ultimate meaning 140, 152, 153, 226
unconditional commitment 152
unconscious 30, 43, 45, 54, 58, 92, 192
Unitarianism 136, 222
unorthodox 51

Vaichinger, H 102
values 24, 26, 49, 53, 54, 58, 67, 68, 70, 90, 108, 128, 132, 133, 136, 141, 143, 153, 154, 164-167, 170, 218, 219, 226, 229, 231, 233, 235